THE
Swing Voter
IN AMERICAN POLITICS

THE

Swing Voter

IN AMERICAN POLITICS

WILLIAM G. MAYER, editor

BROOKINGS INSTITUTION PRESS

Washington, D.C.

ABOUT BROOKINGS

The Brookings Institution is a private nonprofit organization devoted to research, education, and publication on important issues of domestic and foreign policy. Its principal purpose is to bring the highest quality independent research and analysis to bear on current and emerging policy problems. Interpretations or conclusions in Brookings publications should be understood to be solely those of the authors.

Copyright © 2008
THE BROOKINGS INSTITUTION
1775 Massachusetts Avenue, N.W., Washington, D.C. 20036
www.brookings.edu

Library of Congress Cataloging-in-Publication data
The swing voter in American politics / William G. Mayer, editor.
    p.   cm.
  Summary: "Fills conceptual gap concerning the swing voter. Answers four questions: What is a swing voter? How to identify them? Do they differ from the rest of the electorate? What is their role? Presents a picture of this key political group, tracking them across six decades of national and local elections"—Provided by publisher.
  Includes bibliographical references and index.
  ISBN-13: 978-0-8157-5530-2 (cloth : alk. paper)
  ISBN-10: 0-8157-5530-9 (cloth : alk. paper)
  ISBN-13: 978-0-8157-5531-9 (pbk. : alk. paper)
  ISBN-10: 0-8157-5531-7 (pbk. : alk. paper)
  1. Voting—United States. 2. Elections—United States. I. Mayer, William G., 1956– II. Title.
JK1967.S95 2008
324.973—dc22   2007047570

9 8 7 6 5 4 3 2 1

The paper used in this publication meets minimum requirements of the American National Standard for Information Sciences—Permanence of Paper for Printed Library Materials: ANSI Z39.48-1992.

Typeset in Minion and Univers Condensed

Composition by R. Lynn Rivenbark
Macon, Georgia

Printed by R. R. Donnelley
Harrisonburg, Virginia

To the faculty and staff
Department of Political Science
Northeastern University
for their support, friendship, and patience

Contents

Preface

The origins of an idea are usually elusive, rarely capable of being pinned down to a particular time or circumstance. In the case of this book, however, I can say quite precisely when I first became interested in the subject of the swing voter.

In mid-October 2000, while I was reading a morning newspaper, two thoughts suddenly occurred to me. The first was that, in the coverage of the 2000 presidential campaign that I had been reading, watching, or listening to, one of the phrases that seemed to come up most often was the *swing voter*. What were the swing voters looking for? What were the candidates doing to attract the swing voters? Which candidate would the swing voters finally support? These and similar questions were the focus of story after story.

The second thought, however, was that the whole concept seemed to be a rather murky one. There was, so far as I could see, almost no hard information about who the swing voters were or the kinds of attitudes and opinions they held or even what the term meant. Given my academic background, it came as no great surprise to me that reporters and election commentators showed scant interest in theoretical clarity or methodological precision. (We academics are trained to look down on such people.) But at least on the topic of swing voters, academics were on even shakier ground. Though the swing voter concept had clearly become central to the way political practitioners went about their work and a fair number of recent academic books made use of the term, there was, so far as I knew, zero academic literature on the subject. (After a more exhaustive literature search, I finally did discover one book chapter devoted to swing voters, written seventeen years earlier, in 1983.)

This book is an attempt to fill that void. Its chapters, written by both academic political scientists and public pollsters, are devoted to explicating the swing voter phenomenon. In particular, the chapters focus on three central questions:

1. What exactly is a swing voter? What does the term mean and how do swing voters differ from a variety of "near equivalents" such as independent voters or floating voters?

2. How should the swing voter concept be operationalized? In other words, how can we use survey data to determine who is and who is not a swing voter?

3. What, if anything, do we know about swing voters? Are there significant differences between swing voters and the rest of the electorate? Are there particular groups that are over- or underrepresented among swing voters? And what role do swing voters actually play in determining the outcomes of contemporary elections?

Through the good offices of the Carnegie Corporation, we were able to hold a conference, "The Swing Voter in American Politics," at Northeastern University on June 10, 2006, at which earlier versions of these chapters were presented. Most of them have been substantially revised to reflect the questions and criticisms raised at that conference.

We hope that the result provides a firm foundation for continued research on swing voters and, thus, on the workings of contemporary election campaigns.

For their help in putting the Northeastern conference together, I would like to express my gratitude to two groups of people.

The first is the Carnegie Corporation and its staff, particularly Geri Mannion, chair of the Strengthening U.S. Democracy Program and Special Opportunities Fund, for their generous financial support. This project would never have gotten off the ground without the Carnegie Corporation's assistance.

The second is my colleagues in the political science department at Northeastern, who encouraged and supported my efforts every step of the way. A friend of mine who has been a visiting professor of political science at almost every major university in the Boston area says that Northeastern has far and away the most friendly and collegial department. Certainly that has been my experience. I am particularly grateful to John Portz and Janet-Louise Joseph for helping plan and organize the conference, and to Bill Crotty, Chris Bosso, Michael Tolley, and Ron Hedlund for participating in it. A special word of appreciation should be said about Michael Dukakis, who participated in all the planning meetings *and* helped secure the funding for the conference *and* chaired one of the panels. I know I speak for everyone in the department when I say that he is a simply splendid colleague and a model for the way that a former elected official should act when he or she becomes part of an academic institution.

For helping turn the conference papers into a book as smoothly and painlessly as possible, all of the contributors would like to thank Brookings Institution Press, especially Chris Kelaher, Mary Kwak, and Janet Walker, as well as Katherine Scott, who served as copyeditor.

Finally, I would like to thank my family—my wife, Amy Logan, and our children, Natalie and Thomas—for allowing me the time to do my work and for making the time when I'm not doing my work so rewarding.

THE
Swing Voter
IN AMERICAN POLITICS

one
What Exactly Is a Swing Voter?
Definition and Measurement

William G. Mayer

When journalists, commentators, and political strategists talk about elections, few terms come up more frequently than *swing voter*. Every election cycle, there are literally hundreds of articles that speculate or make confident assertions about who the swing voters are, what they want, what the campaigns are or should be doing to attract them, and how they will finally cast their ballots. For all its popularity among reporters and practitioners, however, the concept of the swing voter has been almost entirely ignored by academic analysts of voting and elections. As far as I can determine, there is not a single journal article and just one book chapter devoted to the subject (the exception is Stanley Kelley's *Interpreting Elections* [1983], which I discuss later). Though an increasing number of academic works make use of the phrase, none tries to define it very precisely or to investigate its general properties.

Given the lack of previous work on this topic, a good part of this chapter is taken up with definitional and measurement issues. I first try to explain just what the term *swing voter* means and then suggest a straightforward way of locating swing voters in a mass sample survey, such as the American National Election Studies. I then compare my own definition to some alternative ways of trying to make sense of the swing voter concept. With the definition established, I then make an initial attempt to test some basic hypotheses about who the swing voters are and in what ways, if any, they differ from the rest of the electorate. I conclude with some suggestions about directions for further research.

Defining the Swing Voter

Though popular commentators often make assertions about who the swing voters are and what they believe, the phrase is, not surprisingly, rarely defined very precisely. Still, as terms in ordinary political discourse go, this one is not especially vague or elastic. The definition that follows is partly descriptive and partly stipulative: that is to say, it is designed both to reflect what *most* people seem to mean when they use the term and to suggest what the term *ought* to mean if it is to contribute something new and valuable to the study of campaigns and elections.

In simple terms, a swing voter is, as the name implies, a voter who could go either way: a voter who is not so solidly committed to one candidate or the other as to make all efforts at persuasion futile.[1] If some voters are firm, clear, dependable supporters of one candidate or the other, swing voters are the opposite: those whose final allegiance is in some doubt all the way up until Election Day. Put another way, swing voters are ambivalent or, to use a term with a somewhat better political science lineage, cross-pressured.[2] Rather than seeing one party as the embodiment of all virtue and the other as the quintessence of vice, swing voters are pulled—or repulsed—in both directions.

To make this definition just a bit more concrete, and to point the way toward operationalizing it in a survey of the potential electorate, let us suppose we had a scale that measured each voter's comparative assessment of the two major-party presidential candidates. At one end of the scale—for convenience, let us designate it –100—are voters who see the Democratic standard bearer as substantially, dramatically superior to the Republican nomi-

---

1. As indicated in the text, among media articles that do provide an explicit definition of the swing voter, this is the most common approach. See, for example, Joseph Perkins, "Which Candidate Can Get Things Done?" *San Diego Union-Tribune*, October 20, 2000, p. B-11; Saeed Ahmed, "Quick Hits from the Trail," *Atlanta Constitution*, October 26, 2000, p. 14A; and "Power of the Undecideds," *New York Times*, November 5, 2000, sec. IV, p. 14.

2. Though it never employed the term "swing voter," one antecedent to the analysis in this chapter is the discussion in most of the great early voting studies of social and attitudinal cross-pressures within the electorate. See, in particular, Lazarsfeld, Berelson, and Gaudet (1948, pp. 56–64); Berelson, Lazarsfeld, and McPhee (1954, pp. 128–32); Campbell, Gurin, and Miller (1954, pp. 157–64); and Campbell and others (1960, pp. 78–88). There was, however, never any agreement as to how to operationalize this concept (Lazarsfeld and his collaborators tended to look at demographic characteristics; the Michigan school used attitudinal data); and almost the only empirical finding of this work was that cross-pressured voters tended to be late deciders. For reasons that are not immediately clear, more recent voting studies have almost entirely ignored the concept. The term appears nowhere in Nie, Verba, and Petrocik (1976); Fiorina (1981); or Miller and Shanks (1996).

nee. In other words, these voters have both a highly positive opinion of the Democratic candidate and a very negative opinion of the Republican candidate. Voters located at +100 have a similarly one-sided view of the campaign, albeit one favoring the Republicans. Those at or near zero, by contrast, have a more even or balanced set of attitudes. They may like both candidates equally or dislike them equally. The important point is that voters in the middle of the scale are not convinced that one candidate is clearly superior to the other.

This last group are the swing voters; and it is not difficult to see why they occupy a particularly important place in the thinking of campaign strategists, for as the presidential campaigns set about the task of persuading voters to support their candidate, they are likely to focus their efforts to a great degree on these swing voters, while ignoring or taking for granted voters located near the two end points of the scale.

To see why this is the case, consider the situation of a voter located at −100 or −80 (that is, at the far Democratic end of the scale). The Democrats will probably expend some effort to make sure that this voter will actually show up at the polls on Election Day. But as a subject for *persuasive* actions or communications, this voter is not a very attractive target for either party, simply because there is so little likelihood of changing her voting decision. The Democrats will realize that she is already voting Democratic and thus conclude that, to put it crassly, they have nothing more to gain from her. Even if her ardor for the Democratic candidate cools somewhat, it is most unlikely that she will ever seriously entertain the idea of voting Republican. For similar reasons, the Republicans also have little incentive to spend time or money on this voter. They might succeed in making marginal improvements in this person's comparative assessment of the two candidates, but those shifts are unlikely to have any effect on her final voting decision. Even if the voter moves thirty or even fifty points to the right, she is still positioned solidly on the Democratic side of the scale.

The situation is very different for voters at or near zero. Here, relatively small movements—five or ten points—may have a major impact on a person's vote choice. Hence, voters near zero, the swing voters, will receive a disproportionate amount of attention from both campaigns. As we will see, when American voters are actually arrayed on this sort of scale, the distribution is approximately mound-shaped (it would be stretching things to say that the scale scores are normally distributed), with a somewhat larger proportion of the electorate near the center than are located out on the tails. But even if this were not the case, campaigns would still concentrate on voters in the middle of the scale, because that is where campaigning will have the greatest expected payoff.

The Theoretical Significance of the Swing Voter Concept

Defined in the way I have suggested, swing voters play a potentially significant role in the way political scientists ought to think about elections. The core insight that animates the swing voter concept is that, in the context of an election campaign, not all voters are equal. Voters receive attention from campaigns according to the expected "payoff" they will yield, meaning the number of votes that can be gained or at least not lost to the other side. Thus, campaigns will generally ignore or take for granted each candidate's most committed supporters and concentrate their persuasive efforts on the undecided or weakly committed swing voters. This insight is clearly central to the way consultants and campaign strategists go about their work, even if it has not yet been incorporated into academic models of campaigns and elections.

In this respect, there is an obvious parallel between swing voters and the so-called battleground states in the Electoral College. Like swing voters, battleground states are those that cannot be firmly counted upon to support one candidate or the other, states that are still potentially winnable by either major-party candidate. If one does not take this idea into account, it is very difficult to explain a great deal of what occurs during a presidential general election campaign, such as why the candidates in 2004 spent so little time in California, New York, and Texas, the states with the three largest electoral vote totals, while devoting a lot of effort to considerably smaller states such as New Hampshire, New Mexico, Iowa, Colorado, and Wisconsin. Of course, the analogy between swing voters and battleground states breaks down at several points (all analogies do). For one thing, it is at present much easier to target battleground states than it is to target swing voters, though this may change as we learn more about who the swing voters are and as new campaign technologies permit more precise targeting of individual voters.

The campaigns' focus on swing voters also has normative consequences. Opponents of the Electoral College frequently criticize that institution on the grounds that it leads to a contest in which many states are ignored or taken for granted by both campaigns and so much of the candidates' time and campaign funds is focused on a relatively small number of battleground states. Such a situation, they complain, is manifestly undemocratic, since it makes some voters more important than others. If only we could switch to a direct election system, they say, all voters would be placed on an equal footing.[3]

As the preceding analysis should make clear, however, this last conclusion is manifestly false. A direct election system would undoubtedly remove some existing inequalities, but other types of inequalities would remain and possibly become more important. Campaigns, to put it bluntly, are not for everyone. Those who are already very well informed, those whose ideological and partisan predispositions effectively determine their choices from the moment the candidates are selected—voters of this sort don't need campaigns. And, thus, the distinctive benefits of campaigns—policy commitments adopted during the campaign, special grants and pork-barrel projects from the incumbent administration—will also be distributed unequally.

Operationalizing the Swing Voter

The definition of the swing voter provided earlier can be operationalized very easily. All that is required is a scale that measures, in a relatively nuanced way, each voter's comparative assessment of the two major-party candidates. In the American National Election Studies (ANES), the best way to construct such a scale is with the so-called feeling thermometer questions. In every presidential election year since 1972, the ANES preelection survey has included a set of questions in which respondents are asked to indicate how favorably or unfavorably they view each of the presidential candidates by rating them on a thermometer scale that runs from 0 to 100 degrees.[4] As a number of scholars have shown, these ratings are a meaningful summary indicator of how the respondent evaluates a given person or group and are highly correlated with other important political variables such as voting behavior and ideological self-identification.[5] To determine how a voter compares the two candidates, we need only subtract one candidate's rating from the other's. The scale used in the rest of this chapter was constructed by subtracting the

---

3. See, for example, Longley and Peirce (1999).

4. For reasons that will be made clear, the analysis presented here requires candidate ratings from the preelection survey. Thermometer ratings of the presidential candidates were first included in the American National Election Studies in 1964, but in both 1964 and 1968 these questions were asked only in the postelection survey.

5. See, among others, Weisberg and Rusk (1970); Brody and Page (1973); Conover and Feldman (1981); and Mayer (1996).

Table 1-1. Distribution of Respondents and Division of Major-Party Presidential Vote by Difference in Preelection Thermometer Ratings, 1972–2004

Units as indicated

Difference in thermometer ratings	Percentage of all voters	Percentage voting Democratic	Percentage voting Republican	N
−100 to −91	2.0	100	0	212
−90 to −81	2.8	99	1	300
−80 to −71	0.4	100	0	47
−70 to −61	3.8	99	1	407
−60 to −51	4.7	99	1	505
−50 to −41	5.4	97	3	587
−40 to −31	5.3	95	5	570
−30 to −21	7.1	94	6	767
−20 to −16	4.3	91	9	466
−15 to −11	2.6	85	15	277
−10 to −6	4.5	84	16	486
−5 to −1	0.3	65	35	34
0	8.8	53	47	947
1 to 5	0.3	19	81	32
6 to 10	4.7	19	81	504
11 to 15	2.3	15	85	249
16 to 20	3.9	9	91	420
21 to 30	7.2	6	94	773
31 to 40	5.8	4	96	626
41 to 50	5.5	4	96	598
51 to 60	5.6	1	99	604
61 to 70	5.1	2	98	553
71 to 80	0.6	2	98	60
81 to 90	3.9	1	99	421
91 to 100	3.1	1	99	330
TOTALS	100.0			10,775

Source: American National Election Studies, 1972–2004.

rating for the Democratic presidential candidate from that of the Republican nominee, so that higher scale scores indicate greater Republicanism.

To help anchor the analysis that follows, the first column of data in table 1-1 shows the distribution of these scale scores for all major-party presidential election voters in the nine ANES presidential-year surveys from 1972 to 2004 combined.[6] As has already been noted, the scores are clustered somewhat more densely near the center of the scale, but there are also a surprisingly large number of respondents located at the tails of the distribution.

6. Two general points about the analysis in this chapter should be noted. First, I have followed the lead of virtually every other major academic voting model and treat voting in presidential elections as a dichotomous variable, where voters effectively choose between a Republican and a Democrat. See, among others, Campbell and others (1960, chapter 4); Fio-

Every four years, about one-third of the electorate places the two major party candidates more than 50 degrees apart on the feeling thermometer.

As a simple test of some of the basic points suggested earlier about the nature and utility of the swing voter concept, table 1-1 also shows the division of the two-party presidential vote at every point along the scale for all nine surveys added together. Obviously, the score a respondent gets on this scale is highly correlated with his or her eventual vote. This finding is reassuring but no great contribution to the literature.

What is more noteworthy is what this table shows about the relationship between scale position and "convertability"—the likelihood that a campaign can change a person's vote intention. Since the thermometer ratings in table 1-1 are taken from the preelection survey, whereas the vote variable comes from the postelection survey, one interpretation of these results is that they show the probability that a person who holds a given set of attitudes toward the major-party candidates during the preelection campaign will ultimately cast a Democratic (or Republican) ballot. For voters located at either end of the scale, the odds of effecting a change in their voting intentions are clearly not very great. Of those who place the candidates more than 50 degrees apart during the preelection campaign, 99 percent will end up voting for the favored candidate. Even among those who see a difference of 25 or 30 degrees between the candidates, only about 5 percent will be sufficiently influenced by the campaign to "convert" to the opposition. Only in a rather narrow band near the center of the scale—running from about –15 to +15—does the number of partisan conversions reach 15 percent.

At one level, the data in table 1-1 reinforce a conclusion that academics have long been aware of: that not a whole lot of people change their votes

---

rina (1981); Markus and Converse (1979); and Pomper and Schulman (1975). In principle, one could also examine a second class of "swing voters," who waver between voting for one (or both) of the major-party candidates and voting for a third-party contender, though this would require additional data and analysis that would take us far beyond the main subject of this chapter. Second, again like all of the sources just listed, I distinguish voters from nonvoters on the basis of self-report, counting as a voter everyone who told the ANES interviewer that he or she voted. Though it is widely recognized that this results in an overestimation of the voting population—many people who say they voted are lying or mistaken—in most years there simply is no alternative. However, to make sure that this overreporting does not influence the results presented in this chapter, I have rerun the analysis for 1984 and 1988, when the ANES also included a "validated vote" variable, constructed by checking each respondent's self-report with the records kept by the local board of elections. In general, restricting the analysis to validated voters instead of self-reported voters changes very few figures by more than 2 percentage points and has no effect on any of the major conclusions.

during the general election phase of a presidential campaign. But if campaigns cannot create the world anew, they clearly can change *some* votes—and in a close election, those changes may spell the difference between victory and defeat. More to the immediate point, if vote changes do occur, they are much more likely to occur among those near the center of the scale—among swing voters—than among those located closer to the end points. If it is difficult to persuade someone who rates the Democratic candidate 10 degrees higher than the Republican candidate to cast a Republican ballot, it is far more difficult to convert someone who rates the Democratic standard bearer 30 or 50 degrees above his Republican counterpart.

One advantage of using a scale of this sort is that it provides a nuanced, graduated measure of a voter's convertability or "swingness." For the analysis that follows, however, it will be helpful to have a simple, dichotomous variable that divides voters into two categories: swing voters and nonswing voters. A close inspection of the data in table 1-1 suggests that the best way to define such a variable is to classify any voter with a score between –15 and +15 inclusive as a swing voter, with everyone else falling into the "nonswing voter" category.[7] Outside of this range, more than 90 percent of the respondents voted for the candidate whom they rated as superior in the preelection survey. Within the –15 to +15 range, the defection rate is considerably higher. As shown in table 1-2, by this criterion, 23 percent of the voters in the typical ANES presidential-year survey fit into the "swing voter" category.

There is also, however, some noteworthy variation across elections in the percentage of the electorate who are swing voters. The 1976 election and, to a lesser extent, the 1980 campaign apparently left an unusually large number of voters ambivalent about the two major-party candidates and uncertain whom to support. By contrast, the 2004 election stands out as one in which the electorate was, at least in comparative terms, quite sharply polarized: of those who cast a ballot for Bush or Kerry, only 13 percent could be classified as swing voters.

Some Alternative Definitions

If the definition of a swing voter developed here is plausible and shows some promise of being analytically useful, it is not, I would concede, the only way

---

7. An alternative procedure, less suitable for campaigns but perhaps more appealing to academics, would be to create a composite swing vote by weighting each point on the scale by the probability that a respondent in that position will defect to the opposite party. Experiments

Table 1-2. Major-Party Presidential Voters Classified as Swing Voters, 1972–2004
Percent

Year	Respondents with a score between −15 and +15 on the thermometer ratings scale
1972	22
1976	34
1980	28
1984	22
1988	26
1992	22
1996	18
2000	23
2004	13
Average	23

Source: American National Election Studies, 1972–2004.

of making sense of this concept. In this section, I consider three other ways of specifying what it means to be a swing voter. I do this for two reasons: to suggest why my own definition is better than the alternatives and to demonstrate the validity of the approach developed earlier in this chapter. As will soon become clear, the three alternative definitions considered here are by no means identical with my own conception of the swing voter, but they do get at closely related underlying ideas. If the measurement strategy outlined in the previous section is valid, then its results—in particular, the sorts of people identified as swing voters—ought to be strongly correlated with each of the other variables described here.

Political Independents

If swing voters are those who are not firm supporters of either major-party candidate, who cannot be reliably counted on to march behind either party's banner, perhaps it would make more sense to think of swing voters simply as political independents: as respondents who, in answer to the standard party identification question, express no affiliation with either party. Several political dictionaries actually offer definitions along this line. William Binning, Larry Easterly, and Paul Sracic, for example, define a swing voter as "a term used by journalists to characterize voters that are not strongly attached to

with that procedure show that it yielded results almost identical to those based on the dichotomous variable described in the text.

political parties."[8] A number of media articles on the subject also operationalize the concept this way. Having declared an interest in "swing voters," they examine survey data on or interview people who call themselves independents.[9] But political independence, whatever its other uses, is not a very good measure of what it means to be a swing voter. If the point of the swing voter concept is to identify voters who might conceivably vote for either major-party candidate, political independents fall short in several ways.

On the one hand, there is substantial evidence to show that many self-declared independents are, in fact, "hidden partisans": people who embrace the independent label and the resonances of civic virtue associated with it, but whose actual attitudes and voting behavior are every bit as partisan as those who embrace party labels more openly. This has been shown most exhaustively for the so-called independent leaners, who initially call themselves independents but, when pressed, will concede that they feel "closer" to one party or the other.[10] But even if one looks only at the small residual category—the "pure independents," who account for only about 7 percent of all major-party voters—there is some reason to think that even this group has not been entirely cleansed of hidden partisans. In 1980 and 1984, when the ANES included the party identification question in both the pre- and post-election surveys, between 40 and 60 percent of those who were categorized as pure independents in the preelection survey expressed some level of partisan commitment in the postelection survey. For a number of years, the ANES postelection survey had a question asking respondents if they had voted a straight or split ticket in state and local elections. About a quarter of the pure independents consistently said that they had voted a straight ticket.

On the other hand, not all self-declared partisans can be counted as firm and reliable voters for their own party's presidential candidate. Party identification is a very good predictor of voting behavior, but it is clearly not a perfect one. Every four years, a sizable number of party identifiers, particularly Democratic identifiers, defect to the opposition. On average, between 1952 and 2004, 19 percent of all Democratic identifiers voted for the Republican presidential candidate, while 10 percent of Republican identifiers returned the favor.

8. Binning, Easterly, and Sracic (1999, p. 397); see also Safire (1993, pp. 778–79).

9. See, for example, Jill Zuckman, "Bush: Testing Party, Governor Woos Minorities," *Boston Globe,* July 19, 2000, p. A16; Karen Hosler, "Selection of Lieberman Hailed as 'Bold' Choice," *Baltimore Sun,* August 8, 2000, p. 12A; and Abraham McLaughlin, "Bush and the Momentum Game," *Christian Science Monitor,* September 19, 2000, p. 1.

10. See Keith and others (1992).

Table 1-3. Relationship between Party Identification and Swing Voters,1972–2004
Percent[a]

	Pure independents	Independent leaners	Weak partisans	Strong partisans
Swing voters	40	27	28	12
Nonswing voters	60	73	72	88
		Swing voters	Nonswing voters	
Pure independents		13	6	
Independent leaners		28	22	
Weak partisans		42	31	
Strong partisans		18	41	

Source: American National Election Studies, 1972–2004.

a. Figures represent the average percentages for the nine ANES presidential-year surveys from 1972 through 2004. Difference between swing voters and nonswing voters was significant at the .001 level in each of the nine surveys.

Indeed, in many elections much of the speculation about swing voters— and much of each party's most intensive presidential campaigning—centers on various kinds of partisans who are thought, for one reason or another, to be dissatisfied with their own party's presidential candidate and thus potentially winnable by the opposition. During the 1980s, for example, both parties devoted a great deal of attention to a group popularly known as the Reagan Democrats: white, blue-collar Democrats, most of whom held conservative views on social and cultural issues, who felt increasingly alienated from a party that seemed dominated by blacks, feminists, and other liberal activist groups.[11] If swing voters are defined as political independents, then the Reagan Democrats are simply excluded from this category by fiat, without bothering to investigate their real attitudes and voting proclivities.

Table 1-3 shows the average relationship between party identification and the swing voter for the nine presidential elections held between 1972 and 2004.[12] As one might expect, the two variables are related, but the relationship is nowhere near strong enough to conclude that they measure the same underlying concept. On average, 40 percent of pure independents

11. As with the swing voter, there is some ambiguity as to what exactly a "Reagan Democrat" was. The definition used here seems to be what most people who used the term had in mind.

12. To conserve space and enhance interpretability, tables 1-3, 1-4, 1-5, and 1-8 show only the average of the results from the nine separate surveys. In each case, the results do not vary much from survey to survey. Where there is some danger that averages such as these might hide very different results in individual surveys, as in tables 1-7 and 1-9, I report separate results for each survey.

qualify as swing voters, as compared to 27 percent of independent leaners, 28 percent of weak partisans, and 12 percent of strong partisans. When the data are percentaged the other way, pure independents account for just 13 percent of the swing voters; the modal swing voter, in every survey analyzed here, was actually a weak partisan.

Party Switchers

Another political science category that bears some relationship to the concept of swing voters is that of the party switcher or floating voter: voters who actually cross party lines from one election to the next, who vote for a Republican in one presidential contest and a Democrat in the succeeding one or vice versa. Like party identification, the party switcher variable has a distinguished political science lineage: though not used quite so often in recent years, it was once a major analytical tool in academic voting studies.[13] But party switchers are simply not the same thing as swing voters. There are too many people who fit into one category and not the other or vice versa.

Most obviously, since party switchers are defined by a disjunction in voting behavior across two successive elections, using this variable as a way of identifying swing voters automatically excludes all those who did not or could not vote the last time around. (Since 1972 on average 15 percent of the major-party votes cast in presidential elections have come from people who said they did not vote in the previous election.) Second, the party switcher category leaves out all those voters who thought seriously about voting for a different party than they had four years earlier but finally decided not to. If it is, in many circumstances, worth knowing about the people who switched sides in successive presidential elections, the swing voter concept gets at a slightly different idea: voters who waver between the parties within the confines of a single election campaign, at least some of whom will stick with the party they supported the last time around.

If not all swing voters are party switchers, the reverse is also true: not all party switchers are swing voters. Party switchers include all those who de-

---

13. The distinction between party switchers and "standpatters" was the major dependent variable used by Key in his widely celebrated book *The Responsible Electorate* (1966). Before the "discovery" of party identification, independents were generally defined in behavioral terms, that is, as those who voted for candidates of different parties, either in the same election or across successive elections. See, for example, Eldersveld (1952). Party switchers also played a major role in some of the early work of the Michigan school. See A. Campbell, "Who Really Switched in the Last Election?" *U.S. News & World Report*, March 29, 1957, pp. 62–67; and Campbell, Gurin, and Miller (1954, pp. 11–27). For a good recent examination of the concept, see Zaller (2004).

cided to abandon the party they voted for in the last presidential election, regardless of when they reached that decision. Some voters will not make that decision until the final days of an election campaign, but many, it appears, decide months or even years earlier and are thus effectively removed from the swing voter category by the time the campaign begins. For example, between 1972 and 1976, the Republican share of the total presidential vote declined by more than 20 percent, from 60.7 percent to 48.0 percent, but most of that decline, the evidence strongly suggests, had been consummated well before the 1976 general election campaign got under way. The huge Republican majority of 1972 was dissolved primarily by the impact of intervening events: the Watergate scandal; the recession of 1974–75; Gerald Ford's decision to pardon Richard Nixon. (The simple fact that George McGovern was not the Democratic presidential candidate in 1976 also helped a lot.) Thus, by the early summer of 1976, many erstwhile Republican voters were safely and comfortably in the Democratic camp, with little or no prospect of leaving it. They were, in short, not swing voters.

All of these points are documented in table 1-4, which shows the relationship between party switchers and swing voters for eight of the nine presidential elections held between 1972 and 2004.[14] As in the earlier analysis of political independents, there *is* a clear relationship between the two variables: party switchers, especially those who jumped from one major party to the other, are more likely to be swing voters than the constants or "standpatters" (the latter term is V. O. Key's), who voted for the same major party in two consecutive elections. But only 41 percent of major-party switchers turn out to be swing voters. In other words, a majority of party switchers were no longer "up for grabs" by the time the general election campaign began. Conversely, major-party and third-party switchers combined account for just 29 percent of all swing voters.

The Undecided

Another way to define the swing vote is to equate it with the "undecided vote"—respondents who tell pollsters that they don't know how they are going to vote in the upcoming election.[15] Of the three alternative definitions of the swing vote analyzed here, the undecided category is perhaps closest in

14. The 1984 ANES survey did not include a question asking respondents how they had voted in 1980, thus making it impossible to identify party switchers in that survey.

15. For media articles that adopt this approach, see Andrea Stone, "Lieberman in Pursuit of Swing Voters," *USA Today,* October 27, 2000, p. 8A; Kim Ode, "Still Undecided? Pay Attention to the Issues," *Minneapolis Star Tribune,* October 28, 2000, p. 1E; and Will Lester, "Swing Voters Still Waffling," *Cleveland Plain Dealer,* October 28, 2000, p. 13B.

Table 1-4. Relationship between Party Switchers and Swing Voters, 1972–2004

Percent[a]

	Major-party constants[b]	Major-party switchers[c]	Third-party switchers[d]	New voters[e]
Swing voters	18	41	24[f]	25
Nonswing voters	82	59	76[f]	75
		Swing voters	Nonswing voters	
Major-party constants		54	72	
Major-party switchers		23	10	
Third-party switchers		6	4	
New voters		17	14	

Source: American National Election Studies, 1972–2004.

a. Figures represent the average percentages for the 1972–80 and 1988–2004 ANES surveys. (The 1984 survey did not include a question asking respondents how they had voted in 1980.) The difference between swing voters and nonswing voters was significant at the .01 level in each of the eight surveys.

b. Major-party constants are those who voted for the same major party's presidential candidate in two successive elections.

c. Major-party switchers are those who voted for the Republican candidate in one presidential election and the Democratic candidate in the next election, or vice versa.

d. Third-party switchers are those who voted for a third-party candidate in one election and a major-party candidate in the next election.

e. New voters includes all voters in a given election who did not vote in the preceding presidential election.

f. Based only on results from 1972, 1996, and 2000. In other years, the number of third-party switchers is too small to permit a reliable estimate.

spirit to my own definition. The principal difference, at the theoretical level, is that the swing vote is a slightly broader concept: it includes not only those who are literally undecided but also those who have some current vote intention but are weakly committed to that choice.

Perhaps the most salient feature of the undecided vote in the ANES surveys is how small it is: of those who said that they were going to vote in the November election, just 7 percent, on average, said they hadn't yet decided who they were voting for. One reason so few respondents are recorded as undecided is that those who initially choose this option are generally pushed or "probed" to say who they think they will vote for. (Unfortunately, none of the ANES surveys makes it possible to determine who was pushed and who was not.)

This is only one aspect of a larger problem: it is very difficult to get a clear, consistent, reliable measure of the "undecided vote." Estimates of its size and composition vary a great deal, depending on such factors as the way questions are worded and whether and how interviewers are instructed to deal with respondents who initially claim to be undecided. In an analysis of preelection polls from 1988, for example, Andrew Gelman and Gary King found that variations in question wording had little effect on the relative levels of support expressed for George H. W. Bush and Michael Dukakis. But "the proportion undecided and refusing to answer the survey question varied consistently and considerably with the question wording and polling organization."[16]

There is also some reason to think that many of those who say they are undecided may actually have a preference that they are reluctant to reveal to the interviewer. The strongest evidence on this point comes from the Gallup Poll, which for many years measured voter preferences in presidential elections in two different ways. Half of the sample were asked by the interviewer, in the now-familiar way, whom they would vote for if the election were held today. The other half were given a "secret ballot" listing the major candidates, which they were asked to mark in private and then deposit in a specially marked "ballot box." This simple subterfuge had a significant impact on the size of the undecided vote, reducing it by about a third. In the fall of 1976, when Gallup used the nonsecret method, 17 percent of all respondents initially said they were undecided. When, in a follow-up question, respondents were asked whether they "leaned" toward one candidate or the other, the undecided vote dropped to 9 percent. Among those respondents who used the secret ballot, however, just 6 percent were undecided.[17]

When compared to the supporters of major-party candidates, the undecided vote also appears to be unusually fluid. Large numbers of voters drift into and out of the undecided category throughout the general election campaign. In a panel study of the 1972 presidential campaign in the Syracuse, New York, area conducted by Thomas Patterson and Robert McClure, 13 percent of the respondents were classified as undecided in a September survey, as compared to 11 percent undecided in the October wave. But these relatively stable aggregate figures mask a far larger amount of turnover at the individual level. Of those who said they were undecided in September, 43 percent had settled upon a candidate in October. On the other side, 28 percent of the October undecideds had been classified as Nixon or McGovern supporters in September.

For reasons both conceptual and empirical, then, I think it better to define and measure the swing vote as I have proposed in the previous section of this chapter than to equate it with the undecided vote. Yet if the swing voter definition proposed here is at all valid, the two variables should be

16. Gelman and King (1993, p. 424).
17. See Perry (1979).

Table 1-5. Relationship between Undecided Voters and Swing Voters, 1972–2004
Percent[a]

	Undecided voters	Voters expressing a candidate preference
Swing voters	67	19
Nonswing voters	33	81
	Swing Voters	Nonswing voters
Undecided voters	16	2
Voters expressing a candidate preference	84	98

Source: American National Election Studies, 1972–2004.

a. Figures represent the average percentages for the nine ANES presidential-year surveys from 1972 through 2004. Difference between swing voters and nonswing voters was significant at the .001 level in each of the nine surveys.

strongly correlated—a hypothesis that is amply confirmed by the data in table 1-5. Of those classified as undecided in the ANES surveys between 1972 and 2004, 67 percent, on average, also fell into the swing voter category, whereas just 19 percent of those who expressed a candidate preference were swing voters.

A Different Measurement Strategy

As noted earlier, there is only one other attempt in academic social science that I know of to conduct a systematic investigation of the characteristics and behavior of swing voters. Stanley Kelley's *Interpreting Elections* (1983) is, as its title implies, primarily an effort to develop and apply a general theory about the meaning of presidential elections, but in chapter 8, Kelley focused specifically on the role played by a group he usually called marginal voters, though he did occasionally use the term *swing voters* as well.

Kelley defined marginal voters in a way that is similar to the one proposed earlier in this chapter,[18] but he used a different set of survey questions to operationalize that concept. In every presidential election since 1952, the ANES has included a sequence of eight open-ended questions, which ask

18. Measurement issues aside, Kelley's definition of the marginal voter is slightly different from my own concept of the swing voter. As Kelley defines the term, marginal voters are "that one-fourth of respondents at the intersection of, and equally divided between, the winner's core supporters and the potential opposition majority. The voters represented by these

respondents whether there is "anything in particular" that they like or dislike about the presidential candidates and the two major political parties. For each such question, interviewers are instructed to record up to five distinct comments. By simply counting up all the comments favorable to the Republicans and hostile to the Democrats, and subtracting the total number of comments favorable to the Democrats and unfavorable to the Republicans, Kelley created an index ranging from −20 (for the most zealous supporters of the Democratic candidate) to +20 (for equally zealous Republicans).

Table 1-6 shows the cumulative distribution of respondents on this scale for the eight ANES presidential-year surveys conducted between 1976 and 2004,[19] along with the division of the major-party vote at each point along the scale. As with my own scale, there is a clear and strong relationship between a respondent's position on the Kelley index and his likelihood of voting for the Democratic or Republican candidate. Those with a score of −10 or less are almost certain to vote Democratic, those with a score of +10 or higher are all-but-certain Republican voters, whereas those in the middle are, to some extent, still up for grabs.

Not surprisingly, Kelley's scale and my own are highly correlated. Across the eight surveys analyzed here, the average correlation between the two variables was .82. Yet much of this correlation reflects the simple fact that both scales do a very good job of discriminating between Democratic and Republican voters. From the perspective of the issues addressed in this chapter, a better test of the scales' comparability is to ignore partisan direction by taking their absolute values, and see how well the scales agree in distinguishing between weak and highly committed supporters of the candidates. The correlation between the absolute values of these two scales is, on average, just .49, suggesting a considerable degree of overlap but also a fair measure of disagreement.

Though at one point I considered using Kelley's method as the basis for my own investigation, I ultimately came to believe that it had two major shortcomings. First and most important, the Kelley index, in my opinion,

---

respondents gave the winning candidate the 'last' increment of voters he needed to win, 'last' in the sense that among them was the least enthusiastic segment of his core supporters" (70–71). In a close election, where the two sides are about equal at the start of the campaign, Kelley's marginal voters will be the same as my swing voters. In a landslide election, where one candidate is substantially more popular than the other, the marginal voter category will probably include a number of respondents who are not, according to my criterion, swing voters. In terms of the specific issues addressed in the next few pages, however, this difference is not important.

19. In the 1972 ANES, survey administrators coded only three comments per question, thus making it difficult to compare scale scores from that year with scores for other years.

Table 1-6. Distribution of Respondents and Division of Major-Party Presidential Vote by Net Number of Likes and Dislikes, 1976–2004

Net number of likes and dislikes	Percentage of all voters	Percentage voting Democratic	Percentage voting Republican	N
−20 to −16	1.2	100	0	106
−15 to −11	6.5	99	1	570
−10	2.1	100	0	181
−9	2.7	97	3	235
−8	3.4	97	3	296
−7	3.6	96	4	314
−6	3.9	94	6	339
−5	4.7	93	7	415
−4	5.0	89	11	437
−3	5.2	82	18	460
−2	5.4	79	21	471
−1	5.8	63	37	511
0	7.0	44	56	617
1	5.1	19	81	451
2	5.3	12	88	463
3	5.0	8	92	438
4	4.8	6	94	420
5	4.1	6	94	357
6	3.9	4	96	342
7	3.1	2	98	273
8	3.0	2	98	262
9	2.3	1	99	199
10	1.7	0	100	146
11 to 15	4.5	1	99	397
16 to 20	0.7	0	100	64

Source: American National Election Studies, 1976–2004.

actually measures two things: a respondent's comparative assessment of the major candidates and parties, but also, to some extent, his or her level of political sophistication. That is to say, one can wind up near the center of the Kelley scale in one of two ways: by providing a large number of likes and dislikes that are almost evenly balanced in their support for or opposition to each party; or by having very little at all to say. As a number of scholars have argued, a simple count of the total number of likes and dislikes a respondent provides to the eight questions in the ANES survey is a good measure of political knowledge and awareness.[20] No matter how strongly they support a particular candidate, some respondents simply are not able to offer much in the way of specific things they like about him or dislike about his opponent. Given the rather low number of likes and dislikes recorded for many respon-

20. See, for example, Smith (1989, chapter 2) and Delli Carpini and Keeter (1996, p. 304).

dents—in the eight surveys analyzed here, one fourth of all major-party voters, on average, offered a total of five comments or less—it is likely that many of those classified as marginal or swing voters according to the Kelley index are actually quite sure which candidate they will support, but are not very good at articulating the reasons for their decision. Using the thermometer ratings avoids this confusion.

The other point in favor of the measurement strategy proposed in this chapter is its simplicity. Given the major role that the swing voter plays in a good deal of contemporary writing and thinking about campaigns, it is desirable, I believe, to develop a way of operationalizing that concept that can easily be included in other surveys and extended to other contexts. Whatever its other advantages, a scale like the one Kelley used is plainly not designed for or well suited to such a purpose. It requires too many questions and too much additional time and training from both interviewers and coders. My own scale, by contrast, is built from just two relatively uncomplicated questions.

Swing Voters and Election Outcomes

What role do swing voters actually play in determining the outcome of presidential elections? To answer this question, table 1-7 breaks down the presidential electorate into three major groups: the Democratic base voters, who have thermometer-rating scale scores between −100 and −16; the swing voters, who, as defined earlier, are those with scale scores between −15 and +15; and the Republican base voters, who have scale scores between +16 and +100. The table then shows, for each of the last nine presidential elections, the distribution of the electorate across these categories and the division of the major-party presidential vote within each category. For this table, I have also followed the lead of James Campbell and weighted the ANES data so that the survey results are equal to the actual votes cast, as recorded by state boards of elections.[21]

The base vote, as I am using the term here, is the opposite of the swing vote: it is the voters whose support a candidate can comfortably rely on. On average, the eighteen major-party candidates shown in table 1-7 held on to 96 percent of their base vote. The problem for most campaigns is that the base vote falls short of a majority. Hence, the principal goal of the campaign becomes to add on to the base vote enough weakly committed, undecided, and even initially antagonistic voters to secure a majority. And that, of course, is where the swing vote becomes important.

21. Campbell (2000).

Table 1-7. Swing Voters and Presidential Election Outcomes

Percent[a]

Year	Party	Percentage of all major-party voters	Percent voting Democratic	Percent voting Republican
1972	Democratic base vote	25	96	4
	Swing voters	22	51	49
	Republican base vote	53	6	94
1976	Democratic base vote	32	96	4
	Swing voters	34	54	46
	Republican base vote	34	6	94
1980	Democratic base vote	36	92	8
	Swing voters	27	38	62
	Republican base vote	37	3	97
1984	Democratic base vote	31	97	3
	Swing voters	22	44	56
	Republican base vote	47	2	98
1988	Democratic base vote	32	97	3
	Swing voters	26	55	45
	Republican base vote	42	3	97
1992	Democratic base vote	40	99	1
	Swing voters	22	56	44
	Republican base vote	37	3	97
1996	Democratic base vote	47	96	4
	Swing voters	18	50	50
	Republican base vote	36	2	98
2000	Democratic base vote	39	95	5
	Swing voters	23	52	48
	Republican base vote	38	3	97
2004	Democratic base vote	42	96	4
	Swing voters	13	53	47
	Republican base vote	45	2	98

Source: American National Election Studies, 1972–2004.

a. Data have been weighted so that the survey results are equal to the actual results.

The swing vote is most significant, then, in close elections. The basic dynamic can be seen most readily in the elections of 1976, 1980, 1992, and 2000. In each of these contests, both major-party candidates had a base vote of between 30 and 40 percent of the electorate. When this is the case, which candidate wins will depend on how the swing vote breaks—and in every one of these elections, the candidate who won a majority of the swing vote also won a majority of the popular vote as a whole (though in Gore's case this wasn't enough to carry him into the White House).

The situation is different when the general election shapes up to be a landslide. In 1972, for example, 53 percent of the voters in the ANES preelection survey were already part of the Republican base vote. To win the 1972 election, George McGovern had to win an overwhelming percentage of the swing voters *and* make some substantial inroads into the Republican base. In fact, as the figures in table 1-7 indicate, Nixon held on to 94 percent of his base vote—and also won 49 percent of the swing voters. Ronald Reagan in 1984 and Bill Clinton in 1996 similarly began the general election campaign with a base vote that fell just shy of a majority.

The most one can say about the role of the swing vote in these three elections, then, is that it helped determine the size of the winning candidate's victory. Yet even in an election of this type, both campaigns would probably be well-advised to concentrate most of their efforts on swing voters. From the perspective of the leading candidate, the swing vote may provide him with the final votes necessary to secure a majority—and can also spell the difference between a comfortable victory and a landslide, a difference that most presidents take very seriously. As for the trailing candidate, even though it is most unlikely that he can win 80 or 90 percent of the swing vote, there simply is no better alternative. The swing voters represent the most likely source of converts. After that, the odds only become even more prohibitive.

The 1988 and 2004 elections are more difficult to categorize. In 1988, the Republican base vote was 10 percentage points larger than the Democratic base vote, but the GOP base represented just 42 percent of the major-party electorate and thus left George H. W. Bush well short of a majority. In 2004, as a result of the sharp drop in the number of swing voters, George W. Bush had a base vote of 45 percent, but John Kerry's base vote, at 42 percent, was only slightly smaller. To win the election, in other words, both Republican candidates needed to win a substantial share of the swing vote, but they did not need a majority. In the end, both Bushes carried enough swing votes to win the election, but it was actually their opponents who won a majority of the swing vote.

The swing vote, in sum, is not the be-all and end-all of American presidential elections. It is much less important in landslide elections—but, then, so are campaigns in general. For a candidate in McGovern's position—trailing an incumbent president by about 25 percentage points in most national polls at the start of the fall campaign—there was probably nothing he could have done to avert defeat. Had he run a good campaign, he might have reduced the size of Nixon's victory, but a Democratic win in 1972 was probably never in the cards. But in the more typical case, where an election is close, the final outcome hinges to a great extent on the decisions reached by swing voters.

One final point should be made about the data in table 1-7. The swing voter concept serves a number of useful functions, but one use to which these data should *not* be put is to use the final verdict rendered by swing voters as a measure of which candidate ran the better campaign. To begin with, the ANES preelection interviews generally do not begin until September, by which time many of the best strategic moves and worst campaign blunders have already taken place. In 1988, for example, many analysts believe that Bush won the election primarily because of a series of attacks he launched on the gubernatorial record of Michael Dukakis in mid- to late August and because of Dukakis's failure to reply to those attacks more quickly and effectively. Based on contemporary polling by Gallup and other organizations, it seems likely that Bush's attacks moved a lot of undecided voters to support the vice president and made a lot of Dukakis supporters less comfortable with their choice. But any such effects would not be picked up in the ANES preference data.

In addition, the dynamics of a particular election may produce a swing electorate that is predisposed toward one of the candidates. In 1988, for example, Bush was much more successful than Dukakis in uniting his own partisans around his candidacy during the summer. The result was that of the swing voters in the 1988 ANES sample, 54 percent were self-identified Democrats and only 35 percent were Republicans. With that kind of initial advantage, it is no great surprise that Dukakis ultimately won a small majority of the swing voters.

Who Are the Swing Voters?

Are certain kinds of people more or less likely to be classified as swing voters? Do swing voters, when compared to the rest of the electorate, have distinctive attitudes or demographic traits? These questions are often the focus of journalistic writing about swing voters; they are also an essential issue for a social science analysis of the swing voter concept. Before we develop more elaborate theories about how swing voters decide which candidate to support, we need to establish some basic propositions about who they are. Indeed, all of the attention that campaigns lavish on swing voters—and any attempt to argue that they are theoretically important—presumes that swing voters are, in at least some important ways, different from the rest of the electorate. If swing voters are, for all practical purposes, a randomly selected subset of all voters, then a campaign's decision to concentrate on swing voters will not change its strategy. It will talk about the same issues, in the same ways, and make the same kinds of promises that it would if swing voters did not exist and it was targeting its message indiscriminately to the entire electorate.

Given the hundreds of questions that are typically included in the ANES surveys, it is obviously not my intention to provide an exhaustive, definitive answer to these questions. Instead, based on previous work about ambivalent and cross-pressured voters as well as contemporary journalistic analyses of the swing voter phenomenon, I have developed four major hypotheses about how swing voters might differ from their "nonswing" counterparts.[22]

Hypothesis 1: Swing voters are less partisan than nonswing voters. The evidence for this hypothesis has already been presented in table 1-3. As noted there, in every single survey, there is a large and statistically significant difference, in exactly the direction predicted: swing voters are less partisan.

Hypothesis 2: Swing voters are more likely to be moderates, both in general ideology and on specific issues. Those at the more extreme ends of the ideological spectrum, we might suspect, have a clearer affinity for one of the major-party candidates: liberals for the Democrat, conservatives for the Republican. Moderates, by contrast, are less certain about which nominee better represents their opinions and interests and thus more likely to waver.

At the level of ideological self-description, this hypothesis has a considerable measure of truth. The National Election Studies generally measure ideology on a seven-point scale, ranging from extreme liberals to extreme conservatives. And as shown in table 1-8, swing voters are more likely to come from the center of the scale and less likely to be found on the extremes than are nonswing voters, a difference that is highly significant in every survey. Averaging across the nine presidential elections between 1972 and 2004, just 16 percent of the swing voters located themselves at one of the four outer points on the scale (extremely liberal; liberal; conservative; extremely conservative), as compared to 33 percent of the nonswing voters. Meanwhile, 31 percent of swing voters and 22 percent of nonswing voters placed themselves at the exact center of the scale (moderate).

The relationship between being a swing voter and being a moderate gets a good deal weaker, however, when one examines attitudes about specific issues. If one looks closely at the responses to questions on such topics as job guarantees or the best way to provide health care, swing voters are slightly less likely to be found at the extremes on such issues, more likely to be near the center, but the differences are rather small. Of the sixty-three seven-point-scale questions I examined, in fifty-eight cases the proportion of swing voters who placed themselves at one of the four outer points on the scale was less than the proportion of nonswing voters who gave such answers. But in only

22. See especially Campbell and others (1960) and Kelley (1983).

Table 1-8. Ideology of Swing and Nonswing Voters, 1972–2004

Percent[a]

Ideology[b]		Swing voters	Nonswing voters
1	Extremely liberal	1	2
2	Liberal	4	10
3	Slightly liberal	11	10
4	Moderate	31	22
5	Slightly conservative	18	15
6	Conservative	10	18
7	Extremely conservative	1	3
	Don't know, haven't thought much about it	24	20

Source: American National Election Studies, 1972–2004.

a. Figures represent the average percentages for the nine ANES presidential-year surveys from 1972 through 2004. Difference between swing and nonswing voters was significant at the .01 level in each of the nine surveys.

b. As expressed in responses to a seven-point-scale question.

thirty-two of these fifty-eight cases was the difference statistically significant at the .05 level (using a simple difference of proportions test), and in no case were the differences as large as they were for the general ideology question shown in table 1-8.

Hypothesis 3: Swing voters are less informed about and less interested in politics than nonswing voters. Though he presented small bits of other data, the principal focus of Stanley Kelley's analysis of the role of "marginal voters" in presidential elections concerned their competence—and his findings were quite pessimistic. "Compared to voters generally," Kelley concluded, marginal voters "were on average less well educated, less active politically, less interested in the campaign, less informed, and less attentive to politics."[23] Given what has been said earlier, however, about the problematic character of Kelley's method of identifying marginal voters—particularly the fact that it may also serve as a measure of political sophistication—the whole matter is clearly worth revisiting.

Accordingly, I have compared swing voters and nonswing voters on a variety of measures of political interest, involvement, and information. As it turns out, using the thermometer ratings rather than the likes-and-dislikes questions does make some difference. Swing voters as I have defined them are more involved and more knowledgeable than a comparable group based on the Kelley index (specifically, those with scores between –2 and +2, inclusive). But the differences are in most cases rather modest, and not enough to

23. Kelley (1983, p. 157).

undermine Kelley's basic conclusion. Swing voters, no matter how one defines them, are consistently less involved in and informed about politics than the rest of the electorate.[24]

The gap is widest for questions that relate specifically to the current election. By a substantial margin, swing voters are less likely to say that they are "very much" interested in the current campaign, that they care who wins the presidential election, or that they have participated in various forms of campaign-related activity. The difference is somewhat smaller, however, on those survey items that measure longer-term political predispositions. Twenty-six percent of swing voters say they follow government and public affairs "most of the time," as compared to 36 percent of nonswing voters; 52 percent of nonswing voters were rated as having a very or fairly high level of information about politics and public affairs, versus 42 percent of swing voters.

As a generalization, then, one can say that although swing voters are a bit more difficult to reach than nonswing voters, they are not so isolated or apolitical as to make the campaigner's task impossible. In fact, swing voters watch presidential debates in about the same percentages as nonswing voters and are actually *more* likely to report seeing a political advertisement.

Hypothesis 4: Swing voters are demographically different from nonswing voters. Media stories have assigned a remarkable variety of demographic traits to the archetypal swing voter. Among the groups that are often said to be significantly overrepresented within the ranks of the swing voters are women, the young, the elderly, Catholics, and Hispanics. On the other side of the coin, certain groups, particularly blacks, are often depicted as very firmly attached to one of the parties and thus underrepresented among swing voters.

Common as such assertions are, however, what is particularly striking (at least to a social scientist) is that these claims are generally buttressed by not a shred of hard evidence. To put the whole matter to a test, I have selected ten groups that have seemed, in recent elections, to be politically significant and to be frequently implicated in discussions of the swing voter phenomenon: men, women, whites, blacks, Hispanics, white southerners, Protestants, Catholics, the young (age eighteen to thirty), and the elderly (age sixty-five and over). The simple question that table 1-9 tries to answer is: Are any of these groups relatively more or less likely to be swing voters than one would predict on the basis of their numbers in the voting population as a whole?

---

24. For a more detailed presentation of the data on which these conclusions are based, see Mayer (2007).

Table 1-9. Demographic Characteristics of Swing and Nonswing Voters, 1972–2004
Percent

Year	Swing voters	Nonswing voters	Swing voters	Nonswing voters
	Women		*Men*	
1972	58	54	42	46
1976	57	56	43	44
1980	55	54	45	46
1984	56	56	44	44
1988	59	53	41	47
1992	59	55	41	45
1996	51	56	49	44
2000	53	56	47	44
2004	46	55	54	45
	Whites		*Blacks*	
1972	89	91	9	9
1976	94	88**	5	9**
1980	91	88	8	12
1984	88	90	9	9
1988	86	88	11	10
1992	83	85	14	13
1996	86	88	10	10
2000	80	83	13	9*
2004	63	79**	24	12**
	Hispanics		*White southerners*	
1972	. . .ᵃ	. . .ᵃ	15	19
1976	. . .ᵃ	. . .ᵃ	19	18
1980	. . .ᵃ	. . .ᵃ	25	22
1984	7	4*	20	19
1988	9	7	21	20
1992	11	6**	22	20
1996	8	7	31	25
2000	5	5	17	24*
2004	10	7	16	20

(continued)

The most important conclusion to be derived from table 1-9 is that swing voters are, at least in demographic terms, a very diverse group. Of the eighty-seven survey-groups evaluated in table 1-9, in only sixteen cases is the group significantly over- or underrepresented among swing voters—and in only four cases does the difference reach 10 percentage points. To the extent that swing voters are demographically different from nonswing voters, moreover, their distinctive attributes vary from election to election. The only group that is overrepresented among swing voters in at least eight of nine elections is Catholics.

If there is one group that is most often described as a swing constituency in media stories, it is women. Yet not once in these nine elections do women

Table 1-9. Demographic Characteristics of Swing and Nonswing Voters, 1972–2004
(*continued*)

Percent

Year	Swing voters	Nonswing voters	Swing voters	Nonswing voters
	Protestants		Catholics	
1972	57	66**	35	23**
1976	59	65**	30	23**
1980	63	63	27	22
1984	57	60	32	27
1988	62	63	27	25
1992	57	58	27	23
1996	59	57	27	26
2000	46	55**	37	27**
2004	57	56	21	25
	Young (age 18–30)		Elderly (65+)	
1972	29	27	12	15
1976	26	25	14	19*
1980	24	21	21	20
1984	20	23	17	17
1988	22	15 **	20	18
1992	17	17	22	21
1996	10	13	21	25
2000	16	12	17	21
2004	12	19	14	18

Source: American National Election Studies, 1972–2004.
a. The 1972, 1976, and 1980 ANES surveys each contained fewer than twenty-five Hispanic voters.
* Difference significant (two-tailed) at .05 level.
** Difference significant (two-tailed) at .01 level.

emerge as significantly more likely to be swing voters. To the contrary, in 1996, 2000, and 2004, it was men who were more likely to be swing voters (though the difference never quite achieves statistical significance). Contrary to another common claim, blacks are not dramatically less likely to be swing voters than whites are. The perception that blacks are not swing voters probably derives from the fact that, in every recent presidential election except 1992, at least 80 percent of blacks voted for the Democratic candidate. But the swing voter concept, it is important to emphasize, does not measure how lopsided or equally divided a group's eventual vote totals turn out to be, but how many members of that group were undecided or weakly committed during the general election campaign. To judge by the data in table 1-9, in both 2000 and 2004 a fair number of blacks were, at best, lukewarm supporters of the Democratic candidate and might, with a bit more effort from the GOP, have joined the Republican camp.

Inter-Election Stability

To fill out this portrait of swing voters, one final issue is worth addressing: Is being a swing voter a relatively stable characteristic, such that the same people are swing voters in one election after another, or is there a substantial amount of turnover across elections? Unfortunately, there is only one National Election Study that contains the requisite questions at the proper times: the 1972–76 panel.[25]

Table 1-10 shows the correlation between being a swing voter in 1972 and being a swing voter in 1976. In the words of that old familiar academic refrain, the results show both continuity and change. About 50 percent of 1972 swing voters were swing voters again in 1976. But half of the people who were "up for grabs" in 1972 were part of the Democratic or Republican base in 1976. The 34 percent of 1972 swing voters who were committed Democrats in 1976 is easy to explain: many normally reliable Democrats deserted the party in 1972 because they could not stomach George McGovern, but rejoined it as soon as the South Dakota senator was no longer its presidential candidate. More surprising is the sizable number of voters who vacillated between Nixon and McGovern but were firmly committed to Gerald Ford. To put the results in table 1-10 in perspective, I have run similar analyses of 1972–76 continuity for party identification and ideology. Measured by the size of the gamma coefficients, being a swing voter (gamma = .660) is considerably less stable than party identification (gamma = .910), but just as stable as ideology (gamma = .660).[26]

Concluding Observations

The principal conclusion of this chapter is that swing voters do deserve more attention from students of voting and elections than they have received in the past. The concept can be defined so that it does have a clear meaning and can be readily operationalized in election surveys. It also contributes something new and valuable to election studies, by reminding us that in the context of

---

25. The 2000–04 panel, which Daron R. Shaw analyzes in chapter 4 of this volume, has only a postelection component in 2004. This is fine for his purposes, but my own measure, it will be recalled, requires thermometer ratings from the preelection survey.

26. All results are for major-party presidential voters only. To make party identification and ideology more comparable with the three-category swing voter measure shown in table 1-10, both variables were also collapsed into three categories.

Table 1-10. Relationship between 1972 Swing Voters and 1976 Swing Voters[a]
Percent

	1972		
	Democratic Base	Swing Voters	Republican Base
1976			
Democratic Base	62	34	15
Swing Voters	28	51	30
Republican Base	10	15	55
N	160	158	450

Source: American National Election Studies, 1972–76 panel.
a. Results are for major-party presidential voters only.
Gamma = .660.

an election campaign, not all voters are equal, and that voters will receive attention according to their expected payoff.

It is appropriate, then, to conclude with a few comments about directions for future research:

1. Much more work clearly needs to be done on the differences and similarities between swing voters and nonswing voters. Do the two groups differ in the priority or salience that they attach to various issues? Besides being somewhat more moderate, do swing voters differ in the *direction* of their issue opinions? Are they, at least in some years, more likely to be pro-life on abortion or more in favor of gun control?

2. How do swing voters finally decide which candidate to vote for? Do swing voters use different decision processes than nonswing voters? Do they place heavier reliance on retrospective performance evaluations or on the candidates' personal qualities? Do people who see no major differences between the candidates fall back on their party identification as a kind of "default value" or "standing decision"?

3. The data and analysis in this chapter have been concerned entirely with swing voters in presidential elections. Articles in the popular press that use the term *swing voter* also tend to focus overwhelmingly on presidential elections. This raises an obvious question (dealt with more extensively in chapter 5): Can the swing voter concept be applied to nonpresidential elections such as congressional elections? Perhaps the most significant complication in doing so concerns how to deal with voters who do not know anything about one or both of the congressional candidates. The measurement strategy developed in this chapter requires that survey respondents be able to provide some sort of thermometer rating to both major-party candidates. In presidential elections, only about

1 percent of all major-party voters are unable to meet this standard, but the number would surely be far larger in the typical congressional election. Should these uninformed voters just be added in with those who give equal or almost equal ratings to both candidates? Perhapsbut as Jeffrey M. Stonecash shows in chapter 5 of this volume, uninformed voters are not the same as ambivalent voters, and there may be reasons for keeping the two groups separate.

References

Berelson, B. R., P. F. Lazarsfeld, and W. N. McPhee. 1954. *Voting: A Study of Opinion Formation in a Presidential Campaign.* University of Chicago Press.

Binning, W. C., L. E. Easterly, and P. A. Sracic. 1999. *Encyclopedia of American Parties, Campaigns, and Elections.* Westport, Conn.: Greenwood.

Brody, R. A., and B. I. Page. 1973. "Indifference, Alienation and Rational Decisions: The Effects of Candidate Evaluations on Turnout and the Vote." *Public Choice* 15: 1–17.

Campbell, A., P. E. Converse, W. E. Miller, D. E. Stokes. 1960. *The American Voter.* New York: Wiley.

Campbell, A., G. Gurin, and W. E. Miller. 1954. *The Voter Decides.* Westport, Conn.: Greenwood.

Campbell, J. E. 2000. *The American Campaign: U.S. Presidential Campaigns and the National Vote.* Texas A&M University Press.

Conover, P. J., and S. Feldman. 1981. "The Origins and Meaning of Liberal/Conservative Self-Identifications." *American Journal of Political Science* 25: 617–45.

Delli Carpini, M. X., and S. Keeter. 1996. *What Americans Know about Politics and Why It Matters.* Yale University Press.

Eldersveld, S. J. 1952. "The Independent Vote: Measurement, Characteristics, and Implications for Party Strategy." *American Political Science Review* 46: 732–53.

Fiorina, M. P. 1981. *Retrospective Voting in American National Elections.* Yale University Press.

Gelman, A., and G. King. 1993. "Why Are American Presidential Election Campaign Polls So Variable When Votes Are So Predictable?" *British Journal of Political Science* 23: 409–51.

Keith, B. E., and others. 1992. *The Myth of the Independent Voter.* University of California Press.

Kelley, S. 1983. *Interpreting Elections.* Princeton University Press.

Key, V. O. 1966. *The Responsible Electorate: Rationality in Presidential Voting, 1936–1960.* Harvard University Press.

Lazarsfeld, P. F., B. Berelson, and H. Gaudet. 1948. *The People's Choice: How the Voter Makes Up His Mind in a Presidential Campaign.* 2nd ed. Columbia University Press.

Longley, L. D., and N. R. Peirce. 1999. *The Electoral College Primer 2000.* Yale University Press.

Markus, G. B., and P. E. Converse. 1979. "A Dynamic Simultaneous Equation Model of Electoral Choice." *American Political Science Review* 73: 1055–70.

Mayer, W. G. 1996. *The Divided Democrats: Ideological Unity, Party Reform, and Presidential Elections.* Boulder, Colo.: Westview.

———. 2007. "The Swing Voter in American Presidential Elections." *American Politics Research* 35: 358–88.

Miller, W. E., and J. M. Shanks. 1996. *The New American Voter.* Harvard University Press.

Nie, N. H., S. Verba, S., and J. R. Petrocik. 1976. *The Changing American Voter.* Harvard University Press.

Perry, P. 1979. "Certain Problems in Election Survey Methodology." *Public Opinion Quarterly* 43: 312–25.

Pomper, G. M., and M. A. Schulman. 1975. "Variability of Electoral Behavior: Longitudinal Perspectives from Causal Modeling." *American Journal of Political Science* 19: 1–18.

Safire, W. 1993. *Safire's New Political Dictionary.* New York: Random House.

Smith, E. R. 1989. *The Unchanging American Voter.* University of California Press.

Weisberg, H. F., and J. G. Rusk. 1970. "Dimensions of Candidate Evaluation." *American Political Science Review* 64: 1167–85.

Zaller, J. 2004. "Floating Voters in U.S. Presidential Elections, 1948–2000." In *Studies in Public Opinion: Attitudes, Nonattitudes, Measurement Error, and Change,* edited by William E. Saris and Paul M. Sniderman, pp. 166–212. Princeton University Press.

two

Swing Voters in the Gallup Poll, 1944 to 2004

Jeffrey M. Jones

George Gallup was a pioneer in the field of public opinion research. He made his reputation by using a probability-based sample of the American public to correctly predict that Franklin Roosevelt would win the 1936 election. Gallup met the challenge he issued to the *Literary Digest* poll, which had to that point gained wide acclaim for its massive though non-probability-based samples, with which it had correctly called the 1916 through 1932 elections. The *Literary Digest* poll incorrectly predicted that Alf Landon would win in 1936 by a landslide. Gallup's success in 1936 paved the way for modern polling.

Not only was Gallup a pioneer in polling, he also was a pioneer in the measurement of swing voters. In 1937 he asked the first swing voter question on record, according to a search of the Roper Center's historical public opinion database. In that poll, he asked those who had participated in the 1936 *Literary Digest* preelection poll whether they had changed their vote choice after they mailed in their ballot. Six percent said they had. In 1944 Gallup posed the first swing voter question to a general population sample, asking respondents if they were firm in their commitment or if they could change their minds.[1] Since that time, Gallup has asked some type of swing voter

---

1. In 1940, a Roper Poll asked a swing voter question of a general population sample, but that question asked people whether they might change their minds given certain hypothetical events, rather than simply whether they might change their minds in general.

question in almost every presidential election year and has done so routinely since 1972.

This chapter will review the Gallup Poll's data on swing voters, first showing the history of Gallup's swing voter research in surveys conducted across election campaigns. Gallup's large final preelection polls also allow for an analysis of swing voter characteristics in recent election years. Finally, two Gallup re-interview panel studies conducted following the 1996 and 2004 elections provide insight into what swing voters ultimately did on Election Day.

The history of the Gallup Poll's attempts to identify and measure swing voters makes clear that swing voters are a somewhat elusive group. First, the swing voter group shifts over the course of the campaign—often in inconsistent ways, but usually in response to the peculiarities of a particular campaign season. Second, swing voters typically do not share many observable characteristics, so they are hard to identify at an individual or on a group level. To the extent that there are common characteristics among swing voters, they tend to be attitudinal in nature. But even in the realm of attitudes, there is a diversity in the views of swing voters that makes it difficult to reach general conclusions about them. Finally, there are many challenges faced in finding a precise estimate of the size of this group, with the result that estimates can vary substantially depending on an analyst's definitional criteria, question wording, and survey methodology—not to mention other errors associated with polling more generally.

Gallup's swing voter data indicate that the percentage of swing voters in an election usually declines over the course of the campaign, but not always. Significant third-party candidates or weak incumbents may lead to higher proportions of swing voters. Many swing voters exhibit characteristics typical of those who are disengaged from the political process, but a substantial proportion are engaged and simply cannot choose between what they see as two equally attractive—or equally unattractive—options. Swing voters are more likely to support their preferred candidate than to switch on Election Day, though many decide not to vote at all.

Early History of Gallup Swing Voter Questions

Gallup has a long but not always consistent history of asking swing voter questions. It has asked some form of swing voter survey question during every presidential election campaign since 1944 with the exception of the 1960 election. Over the years, the wording of the questions has varied as different situations called for different measurement approaches. The frequency or timing of swing voter measurement has also varied, though it has become more routine in recent elections. These factors complicate the ability to make comparisons of swing voter proportions across elections, but Gallup data do allow analysts to get a good read on swing voters over the course of an individual presidential election year, something academic surveys typically do not permit.

Gallup takes a direct approach to measuring swing voters. After poll respondents are asked to state their current presidential candidate preference, they are asked some version of a question designed to measure their commitment to that choice. Thus, respondents' classification as swing voters or committed (nonswing) voters is based on their self-reported candidate commitment. To be specific, throughout this chapter, swing voters are defined as comprising three types of voters:

—The undecideds, who have no candidate preference at all

—The "leaners," who initially do not express a candidate preference but when probed by an interviewer say that they lean toward one of the candidates

—Those who express a less-than-firm commitment to their candidate, as revealed by the various questions designed to measure voter commitment

The exact criterion for this last group is, of course, dependent on the question wording, but all Gallup swing voter questions are designed to elicit some sense of voters' commitment to their preferred candidates, if not their likelihood of voting for a nonpreferred alternative. In the analysis that follows, the specific questions Gallup has used over the years are discussed in the chronological order in which they were asked, but for ease of reference and comparison, all ten Gallup swing voter questions are shown in the box "Wording of Gallup Swing Voter Questions, 1944 to 2004."

After Gallup pollsters asked Americans for their preference between presidential candidates Franklin Roosevelt and Thomas Dewey in a May 25 to 31, 1944, poll, they asked the following question: "Is there a fair chance that you may change your mind between now and the election, or are you pretty sure you will vote for [Dewey/Roosevelt]?" That question exemplifies the direct self-report approach Gallup has taken to measuring swing voters. Eighteen percent of Roosevelt voters (9 percent of the total sample) and 14 percent of Dewey voters (6 percent of the sample) indicated they might change their minds, which, combined with the 7 percent of undecided voters, produced an estimate that 22 percent of the potential electorate were swing voters.[2] Gallup

2. For ease of reporting, candidate "leaners" are included with those who have an explicit preference for a candidate. All leaners are placed in the "could-change-mind" category of candidate supporters.

Wording of Gallup Poll Swing Voter Question, 1944 to 2004

1944 and 1948

"Is there a fair chance that you may change your mind between now and the election, or are you pretty sure you will vote for [preferred presidential candidate]?"

1952

"Have you pretty definitely made up your mind on that [preference in the presidential election] or is there a chance that you will change your mind?"

1956

"Do you suppose you might change your mind on this [how you will vote for president] between now and the election—that is, is anything likely to come up which might get you to vote another way?" (This question was also asked in 1952, but only as a follow-up to a "generic" presidential preference question, which asked respondents for their preference between the Democratic and Republican parties rather than the candidates, Eisenhower and Stevenson.)

1964, 1968, 1972, and 1976

"Are you pretty certain now how you will vote this fall, or do you think you may change your mind between now and the election in November?"

1972

"How strongly do you feel about this [preference in the presidential election]—would you say you are almost certain to vote for him, or do you think you may change your mind and vote for the other man?"

1980 and 1984

"Do you strongly support him [preferred presidential candidate] or do you only moderately support him?"

1988, 1992, 1996, 2000, and 2004

"Do you support [preferred presidential candidate] strongly or only moderately?"

1988

"How much of a chance is there that you will vote for [nonpreferred major-party presidential candidate] rather than [preferred presidential candidate]: a good chance, some chance, or no chance whatsoever?"

1992, 1996, 2000, and 2004

"Is there any chance you will vote for [nonpreferred major presidential candidate] in November or is there no chance whatsoever that you will vote for him?"

2004

"Are you certain now that you will vote for [preferred presidential candidate] for president, or do you think you may change your mind between now and the November election?"

Table 2-1. Swing Voter Profile from the 1948 Gallup Polls

Percent

Candidate preference and commitment	U.S. Adults		
	August 13–18	August 20–25	September 2–7
Truman	36	39	38
Certain	(20)[a]	(24)	(23)
Could change mind	(16)	(15)	(15)
Dewey	47	44	46
Certain	(34)	(32)	(34)
Could change mind	(13)	(12)	(12)
Wallace	6	3	4
Certain	(3)	(1)	(2)
Could change mind	(3)	(2)	(2)
Thurmond	2	4	2
Certain	(1)	(3)	(1)
Could change mind	(1)	(1)	(1)
Other or undecided	9	10	10
Total percentage of swing voters	42	40	40

a. Figures in parentheses are subgroups of the basic candidate preference groups.

did not ask a swing voter question again in that campaign, but the tradition of measuring voter commitment was born.

In 1948 Gallup asked the same question three times during the famous Thomas Dewey–Harry Truman election match-up. Perhaps as a portent of Truman's improbable comeback victory, all three 1948 polls showed a fairly high proportion of swing voters—roughly four in ten Americans in each survey (see table 2-1).

As is well known, Gallup incorrectly predicted that Dewey, who led throughout the 1948 campaign, would defeat Truman in the final voting. That led to several changes in the way Gallup approached its election polling, beginning with the 1952 election. Whereas previous election polling reported the preferences of all U.S. adults, in 1952 Gallup began to report the preferences of only registered voters throughout the campaign and then, in the final preelection poll, those of likely voters. Gallup also continued its preelection polling closer to Election Day, whereas in 1948 and earlier the final preelection poll results were finished more than a week before voters cast their ballots and thus could miss late movement in the electorate. Gallup asked just a single swing voter question in 1952, with a slightly different wording than had been used in the previous two elections: "Have you pretty definitely made up your mind on that [your preference in the election], or is there a chance that

Table 2-2. Swing Voter Profile from the 1952 Gallup Poll

Percent

Candidate preference and commitment	Registered voters
Eisenhower	50
Definitely made up mind	(35)[a]
Could change mind	(15)
Stevenson	45
Definitely made up mind	(32)
Could change mind	(13)
Other or undecided	5
Total percentage of swing voters	33

a. Figures in parentheses are subgroups of the basic candidate preference groups.

you will change your mind?"[3] As shown in table 2-2, about a third of registered voters could be classified as swing voters on the basis of the data from that poll.

The 1956 election involved a rematch between Eisenhower and Stevenson, but Gallup asked voters a slightly different swing voter question than it had in 1952: "Do you suppose you might change your mind on this [how you will vote for president] between now and the election—that is, is anything

Table 2-3. Swing Voter Profile from the 1956 Gallup Polls

Percent

Candidate preference and commitment	Registered voters	
	August	September
Eisenhower	52	48
Definitely made up mind	(40)[a]	(36)
Could change mind	(12)	(12)
Stevenson	41	43
Definitely made up mind	(32)	(33)
Could change mind	(9)	(10)
Other or undecided	8	9
Total percent swing voters	29	31

a. Figures in parentheses are subgroups of the basic candidate preference groups.

3. Gallup did ask another swing voter question in 1952, but only as a follow-up to a "generic" presidential ballot question that asked respondents for their preference between the Republican and Democratic parties rather than their preference between the candidates Eisenhower and Stevenson, as is the usual practice. For this reason, and because the results of the generic question differed from a candidate-preference question included in the same survey, the data from this second swing voter question are not included in table 2-2.

Table 2-4. Swing Voter Profile from the 1964 Gallup Polls
Percent

Candidate preference and commitment	Registered voters	
	July	August
Johnson	59	64
Certain	(44)[a]	(51)
Could change mind	(15)	(13)
Goldwater	32	25
Certain	(23)	(20)
Could change mind	(9)	(5)
Other or undecided	9	11
Total percentage of swing voters	33	29

a. Figures in parentheses are subgroups of the basic candidate preference groups.

likely to come up which might get you to vote another way?" This question was asked twice in that election, and only about three in ten voters were not firmly committed to one of the candidates in August and September. That relatively low proportion of swing voters may be a result of the match-up between two well-known candidates.

Surprisingly, Gallup did not ask any swing voter questions during the close, hotly contested election of 1960. The practice resumed for good with the 1964 election, however, and a new question was used that was similar in concept to the ones asked earlier: "Are you pretty certain now how you will vote this fall, or do you think you may change your mind between now and the election in November?" With popular incumbent Lyndon Johnson seeking reelection, there were not many swing voters to be found in 1964. In fact, in both measurements (see table 2-4), there were more committed Johnson supporters than there were *total* Goldwater voters (swing and nonswing). By August, Gallup found that a majority of registered voters, 51 percent, were "pretty certain" they would vote for Johnson.

Gallup measured swing voters much later in the 1968 campaign than had been the case in most previous elections. Three times after Labor Day, Gallup asked registered voters the question introduced in 1964, "Are you pretty certain now how you will vote this fall, or do you think you may change your mind between now and the election in November?" (see table 2-5). The 1968 election was closely contested and included a significant third-party challenger in George Wallace. More than one in four registered voters were up for grabs after Labor Day that year.

Table 2-5. Swing Voter Profile from the 1968 Gallup Polls

Percent

Candidate preference and commitment	Registered voters		
	September 19–24	September 26–October 1	October 17–22
Nixon	42	42	42
Certain	(33)[a]	(31)	(31)
Could change mind	(9)	(11)	(11)
Humphrey	29	27	35
Certain	(21)	(20)	(28)
Could change mind	(8)	(7)	(7)
Wallace	22	21	16
Certain	(17)	(16)	(13)
Could change mind	(5)	(5)	(3)
Other or undecided	7	10	7
Total percentage of swing voters	29	33	28

a. Figures in parentheses are subgroups of the basic candidate preference groups.

Swing Voters, 1972 to 1988

The 1972 election can be considered a significant milepost in Gallup's measurement of swing voters. That year, Gallup asked its swing voter questions at regular and meaningful points of the campaign—after each party's convention, in late September, and for a final time in mid-October. As shown in figure 2-1, shortly after the 1972 Democratic National Convention, which nominated George McGovern for president, 44 percent of registered voters were classified as swing voters. That percentage dropped dramatically to 29 percent following the Republican convention in mid-August, which renominated Richard Nixon.[4] However, the percentage of committed Nixon voters actually declined in the period between the Republican National Convention and the election. That did not present a problem for Nixon, who, like Johnson in 1964, could claim more committed voters than his opponent could claim total supporters: for example, in the October poll, Nixon led 60 percent to 32 percent, with 51 percent of registered voters saying they were "pretty certain" to support

4. There was also a slight change in the wording of the swing voter question between early and late August 1972. In the former poll, Gallup asked voters if they were "almost certain" to vote for their preferred candidate; in late August, September, and October, respondents were asked whether they were "pretty certain" to vote for their candidate. It is unclear how much of the change between early and late August can be attributed to the change in question wording.

Figure 2-1. Swing and Committed Voters as a Percentage of Registered Voters, 1972 Gallup Polls

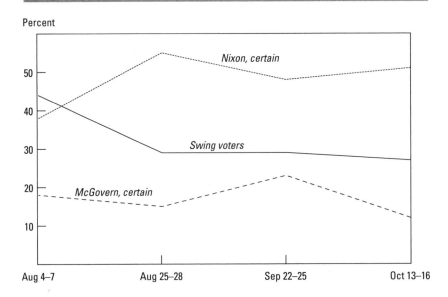

Nixon. The 1972 data suggest that the group of "certain" voters is more fluid than one might expect, even in an uncompetitive election. Many voters who say they are committed to a candidate at one point in the election year may wind up on the fence later in the campaign.

In 1976, Gallup again asked swing voter questions on a regular schedule, including questions in surveys conducted immediately after the Republican convention, then just prior to Labor Day, and then shortly after each of the three Jimmy Carter–Gerald Ford debates. The proportion of all swing voters dropped significantly after Labor Day, from 39 percent to 33 percent, and again following the final debate, from 32 percent to 27 percent (see figure 2-2). The 1976 data also suggest that a lot of the swing voters ended up in the Ford camp. While the number of committed Carter voters stayed fairly constant throughout the late summer and fall, hovering between 34 and 38 percent, the percentage of committed Ford voters steadily increased from 22 percent in late August to 32 percent in late October. The Carter-Ford gap closed even further in Gallup's final preelection poll, which showed Carter and Ford in a statistical dead heat.

Figure 2-2. Swing and Committed Voters as a Percentage of Registered Voters, 1976 Gallup Polls

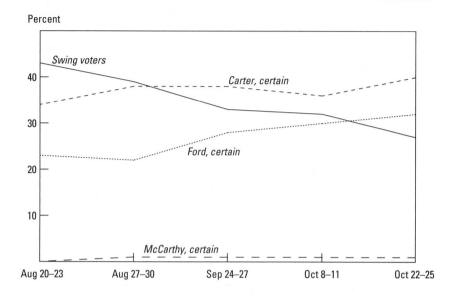

Percent

In 1980, Gallup made another change in the way it measured swing voters. Rather than asking Americans whether they might change their minds about the candidate they were supporting, Gallup asked Americans whether they supported their preferred candidate "strongly" or "only moderately." This would become the standard swing voter question for the next few elections. Indeed, Gallup continues to measure strength of candidate support, though on a less frequent basis and as a complement to rather than a substitute for questions about voters' likelihood of switching their preference.

It is clear that the strength-of-support approach to measuring swing voters differs from the "Will you change your mind?" method. The 1980 data, as set forth in figure 2-3, show a much higher percentage of swing voters (defined as those who are undecided, lean to a candidate, or support the candidate only moderately) than Gallup had found in earlier years: roughly seven in ten registered voters could be so classified using this definition. The high proportion of swing voters in 1980 is probably due to the fact that the strength-of-support question measures two aspects of voter attitudes—their changeability but also the level of enthusiasm for the preferred candidate. For example, in 1980 many

Figure 2-3. Swing and Committed Voters as a Percentage of Registered Voters, 1980 Gallup Polls

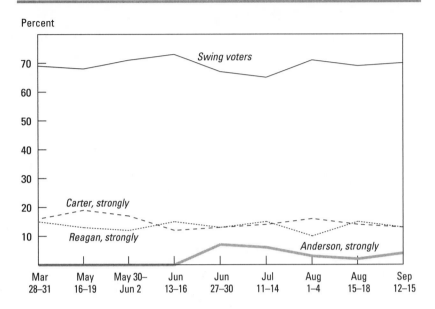

Democrats may have been certain they were going to vote for Carter, but were not thrilled about doing so, given the general perception that he had been an ineffective president. Many Republicans may have had similar reservations about Reagan, who had run unsuccessfully for the party's presidential nomination on two previous occasions and whom many considered too extreme. In fact, majorities of Carter, Reagan, and John Anderson voters all said they were only moderate supporters of their candidate. Throughout much of the campaign, moderate supporters of Carter and Reagan outnumbered strong supporters by about 2 to 1 or more. From March through September of the election year, neither major-party candidate reached 20 percent strong support.

Gallup used the strength-of-support question again in 1984. As shown in figure 2-4, the percentage of swing voters was much lower in 1984 than in 1980 and declined as the campaign wore on. In a shift from 1980, Reagan voters were at least as likely to support him strongly as to support him moderately, as the economy improved and Reagan's approval rating increased along with it. Mondale supporters tended to show weaker support for their candidate, until October, when his strong supporters finally started to outnumber his moderate supporters.

Figure 2-4. Swing and Committed Voters as a Percentage of Registered Voters, 1984 Gallup Polls

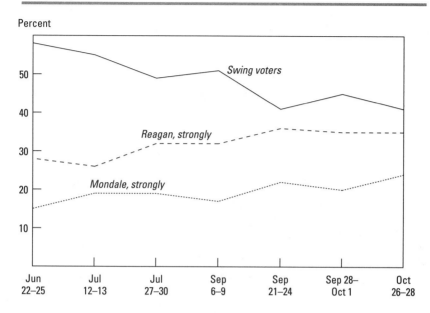

Percent

Gallup continued asking the strength-of-support question during the 1988 campaign, beginning in September of that year. As can be seen in figure 2-5, the proportion of swing voters in the electorate was higher than in 1984. The proportion declined in the spring and summer months, and then was quite stable from Labor Day through Election Day. Another shift that occurred in the fall was that strong George H. W. Bush supporters began to outnumber strong Michael Dukakis supporters as the momentum of the campaign turned in Bush's favor.

During the 1988 campaign, Gallup also renewed the practice of asking voters more directly whether they were likely to change their minds. This was done three times that year (see figure 2-6) and used another new question wording: "How much of a chance is there that you will vote for (the other major-party candidate) instead of (the preferred candidate): a good chance, some chance, or no chance whatsoever?" (Swing voters are defined here as all undecideds, leaners, and those who said there was at least "some chance" that they might vote for the other candidate.)

Since the new question was asked in the same polls as the strength-of-support question, the two sets of numbers can be compared directly (putting

Figure 2-5. Swing and Committed Voters as a Percentage of Registered Voters, 1988 Gallup Polls

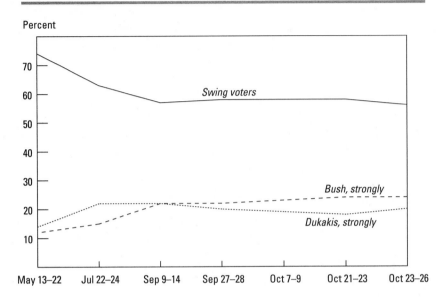

Percent

aside any possible bias in the estimates due to question order). This is done in table 2-6. In general, the new wording produced a much lower estimate of swing voters. For example, in the October 23–26 poll, the how-much-of-a-chance question resulted in 29 percent swing voters as compared to 56 percent using the strength-of-support question. And while the strength-of-support question showed a greater proportion of weak than strong supporters of both candidates throughout the campaign, the how-much-of-a-chance wording showed the opposite, even in May. As indicated earlier, many voters who are not very enthusiastic about their candidate nevertheless say that they will not defect to the other candidate.

Contemporary History

In 1992, Gallup joined forces with CNN and *USA Today* to undertake regular election polling. The CNN/*USA Today*/Gallup partnership led to a substantial increase in the amount of polling done by the Gallup Organization. Gallup's broadcast and print media partners showed a strong commitment to the measurement of swing voters as media attention focused on this group as

Figure 2-6. Swing and Committed Voters as a Percentage of Registered Voters, 1988 Gallup Polls

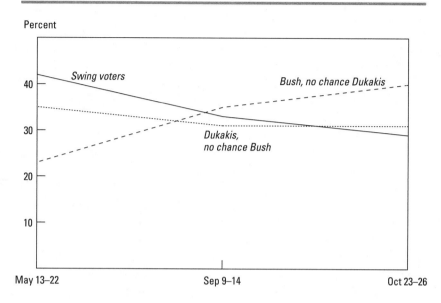

Table 2-6. Comparison of Swing and Committed Voters Using Two Different Wordings of the Swing Voter Question

Percent

Candidate preference and commitment	Registered voters		
	May 13–22	September 9–14	October 23–26
Bush	40	49	52
No chance Dukakis	(23)	(35)	(40)
Some chance Dukakis	(17)	(14)	(12)
Strongly support Bush	(12)	(22)	(24)
Moderately support Bush	(28)	(27)	(28)
Dukakis	53	41	41
No chance Bush	(35)	(31)	(31)
Some chance Bush	(18)	(10)	(10)
Strongly support Dukakis	(14)	(22)	(20)
Moderately support Dukakis	(39)	(19)	(21)

Source: Gallup Poll, 1988.
a. Figures in parentheses are subgroups of the basic candidate preference groups.

a significant factor in elections. The swing voter question Gallup used in 1992 was a slight modification of the question asked in 1988, and was included in every night of CNN/*USA Today*/Gallup's daily election tracking poll, which ran from late September through the eve of Election Day. The new question asked voters who did not support a particular candidate whether there was "any chance you will vote for him, or is there no chance whatsoever." Thus, Bush voters were asked if there was any chance they would vote for Bill Clinton and, separately, for Ross Perot, and Perot voters were asked about the possibility of their voting for Clinton or Bush. In all, there were twenty-two measurements of swing voters using the new question, including several measurements taken prior to the beginning of the daily tracking program. For ease of reporting purposes, the data from the early tracking phase (September 28 to October 26) are combined into weekly averages.

What is clear from the data in figure 2-7 is the effect that Ross Perot's independent candidacy had on voters' commitments. Just over one in three registered voters were classified as swing voters in March, when Clinton was poised to clinch the Democratic nomination and take on the incumbent Bush. Later in the spring, when Perot entered the race and actually reduced Clinton to third-place status, the percentage of swing voters nearly doubled, to 66 percent. Roughly two in three registered voters continued to be classified as swing voters until Perot dropped out of the campaign during the Democratic convention, when the percentage of swing voters was cut nearly in half, to 34 percent. At that time, solid Clinton support more than tripled, from 13 percent to 44 percent, while solid Bush support declined a little, dropping from 27 percent to 22 percent. When Perot reentered the campaign in the fall, the percentage of swing voters increased sharply, from 26 percent to 44 percent, even though he only scored high single-digit support when he first got back into the race. Perot's presence resulted in nearly four in ten voters being up for grabs in late October, in part because the vast majority of Perot supporters were not solidly committed to him and thus were swing voters. Though the swing voter percentage declined in the final days of the campaign, one in three registered voters remained in the swing voter category in the final preelection poll, on November 1 and 2.

In 1992, Gallup for the first time applied a "likely voter" model to its presidential preference data about a week prior to Election Day. As a result, data are available showing the percentage of swing voters among both registered and likely voters in surveys conducted between October 25 and November 2. These surveys, which are reported in table 2-7, repeatedly show that the pro-

Figure 2-7. Swing and Committed Voters as Percentage of Registered Voters, 1992 Gallup Polls

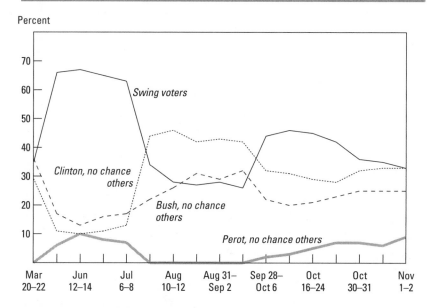

Percent

portion of registered voters who were classified as swing voters was a couple of percentage points higher than the proportion of likely voters who merited this designation. There is typically an even higher percentage of swing voters among all national adults than among registered voters or likely voters. This suggests that estimates of the percentage of swing voters in the electorate depend on how the electorate is defined. It also indicates that Americans who are more involved in the political process are less likely to be swing voters.

In 1996, Gallup did not track swing voters daily as it had in 1992, but still measured them a total of eight times during the campaign, all of which are shown in figure 2-8. Clinton enjoyed a large lead throughout the campaign, so there was not as much drama about the outcome as in 1992. Clinton's support was more solid in 1996 than in 1992, although this increased strength of support was not as dramatic as it had been for Reagan in 1984 compared with 1980. The percentage of swing voters was fairly constant throughout 1996, ranging from the high thirties to the low forties until the end of the campaign. As in 1992, Perot's support in 1996 was largely composed of swing voters. Notably, there were as many swing voters (33 percent of registered

Table 2-7. Estimates of Swing Voters Based on Registered and Likely Voters, 1992 Gallup Polls

Percent

	Swing voter proportion of . . .	
	Registered voters	Likely voters
October 25–26	43	41
October 26–27	43	41
October 27–28	43	40
October 28–29	41	37
October 29-30	37	33
October 30-31	36	33
October 31–November 1	35	31
November 1–2	33	31

voters) in the final days of the 1996 campaign, which resulted in an easy Clinton win, as there had been during the more closely contested 1992 election.

For the 2000 election, Gallup decided to use its likely voter model throughout the campaign, starting in January 2000. The results in figure 2-9, however, are reported for registered voters to maintain comparability with earlier years. The "any chance/no chance" question asked in 1992 and 1996 continued to be used to identify swing voters. Even though 2000 was a much closer election than the Clinton victory in 1996, there were fewer swing voters. Whereas roughly four in ten registered voters were swing voters throughout most of 1996, only about three in ten fell into the swing voter category in 2000. Ross Perot's independent candidacy in 1996 was more substantial than Ralph Nader's and Pat Buchanan's candidacies in 2000, and this accounts for much, but not all, of the difference.

Measurement of swing voters in 2000 was complicated after Labor Day, because the swing voter questions were only asked of Bush and Gore supporters, even though Nader's and Buchanan's names were read to respondents in the vote preference question. The data in figure 2-9 do not count any Nader or Buchanan supporters as swing voters, but if the experience of past third-party candidates is any indication, most people who expressed an intention to vote for either of these two men were probably swing voters.

The data from 2000 once again call into question just how committed the nonswing voters really are. In the August 11–12 poll, conducted after the Republican convention and before the Democratic convention, 42 percent of registered voters were George W. Bush voters who said there was no chance they would vote for Al Gore, but that was the high point in committed voters

Figure 2-8. Swing and Committed Voters as a Percentage of Registered Voters, 1996 Gallup Polls

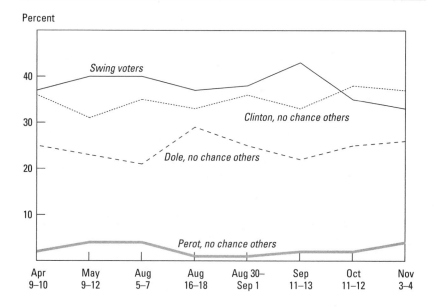

Percent

Apr 9–10 · May 9–12 · Aug 5–7 · Aug 16–18 · Aug 30–Sep 1 · Sep 11–13 · Oct 11–12 · Nov 3–4

for Bush in the campaign. As Bush's large postconvention lead dissipated, his core of committed voters shrank to as low as 30 percent in early September.

During the 2004 election, the "any chance/no chance" question was asked once, in June, but the results from that one survey clearly suggest that fewer voters were up for grabs in 2004 than in almost any previous election. In June 2004, just 20 percent of registered voters could be classified as swing voters. In the spring and summer of 1992 and 1996, when the same question was asked, at least 40 percent of registered voters were swing voters. In the spring of 2000, 29 percent were.

Through most of the 2004 campaign, however, Gallup reverted to a question more like the ones it had used in the 1960s and 1970s: "Are you certain now that you will vote for [Bush/Kerry], or do you think you may change your mind between now and the November election?" The decision to use this wording was made because of several possible shortcomings with the question wording that had been used between 1992 and 2000. In particular, the "any chance/no chance" question was more difficult to interpret in a race where there were several minor candidates on most state ballots. For example,

Figure 2-9. Swing and Committed Voters as a Percentage of Registered Voters, 2000 Gallup Polls

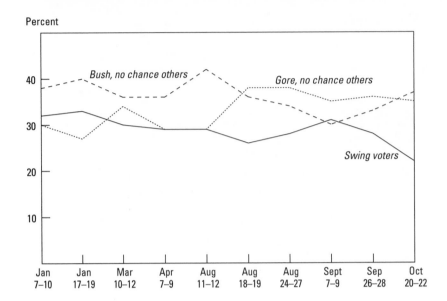

Percent

a John Kerry supporter who said there was no chance that he or she would vote for George Bush might still consider voting for Ralph Nader.

Regardless of the wording used, however, there were not many voters up for grabs in 2004. Through most of the year, when voters were asked whether they were "certain" to vote for the candidate they currently supported, fewer than one voter in four said they might change their minds, and fewer than one in five were swing voters after Labor Day (see figure 2-10). In Gallup's final preelection poll, just 11 percent of registered voters and 9 percent of likely voters lacked a solid commitment. This may be a reflection of the higher voter interest in the 2004 election, which was manifested in the unusually high turnout that year.

Who Are the Swing Voters?

Do swing voters have distinctive demographic or political characteristics? Are certain groups more likely to be swing voters than others?

Demographic characteristics. An analysis of the characteristics of swing voters from late October and early November polls in the elections of 1996

Figure 2-10. Swing and Committed Voters as a Percentage of Registered Voters, 2004 Gallup Polls

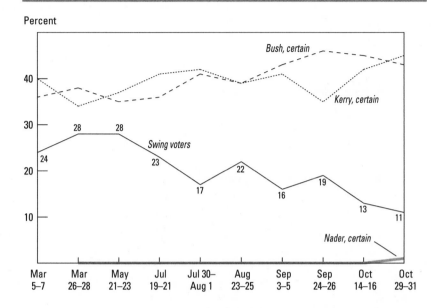

Percent

through 2004 shows that there are no consistent demographic differences across the three elections (see table 2-8). Although significant group-based differences do exist in individual elections, they tend not to hold in other elections. For example, younger voters were more likely than senior citizens to be swing voters in 1996 and 2000, but less so in 2004. Blacks were more likely than whites to be swing voters in each of the three elections, but the differences were fairly minor except in 2000. Thus, it does not appear that people with certain demographic characteristics are more likely to show greater levels of uncertainty about their vote choice across a series of elections.

Political characteristics. There are, however, consistent and sizable differences in the likelihood that Americans with certain political or attitudinal characteristics will be swing voters. Most notably, as can be seen in table 2-9, political independents are roughly twice as likely to be swing voters as Democrats or Republicans. The differences are even greater when one looks at independents who do not express a leaning toward either party. In each of the last three elections, a majority of these "pure" independents have been swing voters.

Political moderates are more likely to be swing voters than are liberals or conservatives, though the difference is not as great as that between those who

Table 2-8. Swing Voters by Demographic Group, 1996–2004

Percent[a]

Group	1996	2000	2004
Men	31	24	11
Women	29	29	12
18–29 years old	34	30	10
30–49 years old	33	28	11
50–64 years old	25	26	10
65 years and older	25	23	14
White	30	25	11
Black	34	36	14
High school or less	30	28	16
Some college	31	28	9
College graduate	29	25	7
Urban	26	30	9
Suburban	31	25	11
Rural	35	28	16
East	29	27	13
Midwest	30	30	14
South	32	28	9
West	28	23	10
Married	28	. . .	10
Not married	33	. . .	13
Children under 18	34	. . .	. . .
No young children	28	. . .	. . .
Live in union household	. . .	. . .	8
Nonunion household	. . .	. . .	12

Source: Gallup Poll, 1996–2004.

a. Cells with ". . ." indicate not applicable. Question not asked that year.

have no party affiliation and those who do. Americans who are engaged in the political process are also less likely to be swing voters than those who are not engaged. In each election, those who said they had given "a lot of thought" to the election were about half as likely to be swing voters as those who had not thought as much about the election. There is a weaker relationship between past voting participation and the likelihood of being a swing voter.

In addition to being less engaged in the political process, swing voters may also be more conflicted or "cross-pressured." The likelihood of an individual's being a swing voter is much greater among those who view both major-party candidates—or neither major-party candidate—favorably. Those who only view one candidate favorably are not likely to be conflicted and, not surprisingly, are less likely to be on the fence.

Table 2-9. Swing Voters by Political Group, 1996–2004

Percent

Group	1996	2000	2004
Democrat	22	25	8
Independent	44	40	22
Republican	27	14	6
Non-leaning independent	56	63	58
Liberal	27	21	7
Moderate	33	37	16
Conservative	28	20	8
Voted in last election	30	24	11
Did not vote in last election	34	38	13
Have thought a lot about election	28	22	10
Have not thought a lot about election	40	42	22
Favorable to both Democratic and Republican candidates	52	59	33
Favorable to one candidate	27	13	5
Not favorable to either candidate	62	59	62

Source: Gallup Poll, 1996–2004.

Are swing voters more likely to be conflicted in a positive or a negative manner? That is, do most swing voters view both candidates favorably and are trying to decide which is the better of two attractive options, or do they view both unfavorably and are they trying to decide which is the lesser of two evils? The answer depends on the election. In 1996, swing voters were slightly more likely to rate both Clinton and Dole favorably (25 percent) than to rate both negatively (19 percent). In 2000, when there was no incumbent candidate, swing voters were three times more likely to be deciding which candidate they liked better (51 percent) than which they hated less (17 percent). The 2004 election presented a different picture, with more swing voters deciding between the lesser of two evils (34 percent) than the better of two attractive alternatives (26 percent).

Table 2-9 only shows data for registered voters, so it does not take into account differences in registration status between swing voters and committed voters. Gallup data show that among eligible adults, swing voters are far less likely to be registered than committed voters are. In 2004, for example, 92 percent of committed voters said they were registered, compared to 74 percent of swing voters. Looking at this in a different way, swing voters were three times more likely to be found in the group of unregistered voters (33 percent) than in the pool of registered voters (11 percent). This is further evidence that many swing voters are disengaged from the political process.

In theory, voters could lack commitment to a candidate either because they lack the information to make a decision or because they have the necessary information but are conflicted and are having difficulty making a choice. Clearly, many swing voters fit the former profile: many are not registered to vote, and those who are registered are less likely to be thinking about the election. However, not all swing voters can be described this way: a significant percentage do have some connection to the political process in that they are registered, are thinking about the election, have some partisan preference, and have voted in the past.

Issue differences. In addition to attitudinal factors, the issues that are salient in a particular campaign may cause some voters to fall into the swing voter group. Unfortunately, the data that allow this possibility to be explored are limited.

In 2000, swing voters were somewhat more likely to say that leadership qualities were more important in their choice of a presidential candidate than their agreement with that candidate on the issues (44 percent to 40 percent). Committed voters said issue agreement was more important by a 45 percent to 35 percent margin. This relationship did not hold in 2004, however, as both swing voters and committed voters said leadership was more important than issues.

Looking at specific issue controversies, in 2004 swing voters were more likely to say health care was the most important issue to their vote (27 percent) than either committed Bush voters (9 percent) or committed Kerry voters (20 percent). Otherwise, swing voters more closely resembled core Kerry voters than core Bush voters, in that they perceived domestic issues such as the economy to be more important than international issues such as the war in Iraq and terrorism. Swing voters were more dissatisfied with the state of the nation in 2004 than committed voters and were somewhat more likely to view the United States as having made a mistake in sending troops to Iraq.

What Becomes of Swing Voters?

From a practical perspective, the main reason to study swing voters is that their final choices can determine the election outcome. In 1996 and 2004, Gallup conducted postelection panel studies in which respondents from its final preelection polls were re-interviewed after Election Day. The data from these interviews, which are reported in table 2-10, cannot address the behavior of those who were swing voters at some earlier point in the campaign but then became committed voters before the final days of the campaign, but they

Table 2-10. Voting Behavior of Swing Voters, 1996 and 2004 Postelection Panels[a]

Percent	1996	2004
Voted for preferred candidate	36	30
Voted for another candidate	8	10
Was undecided, voted for a candidate	7	8
Did not vote	42	33
Cannot determine (refused on pre- or post-interview; missing data)	7	19

Source: Gallup Poll, 1996 and 2004.
a. Based on all swing voters, regardless of registration status or likelihood of voting

do tell us what happens to the most uncommitted voters—those who still do not have a strong preference a few days before they are called on to vote.

The 2004 postelection panel shows that swing voters were more likely to vote for the candidate they preferred than to change their minds.[5] Thirty percent of Americans who were identified as swing voters prior to the election voted for the candidate they preferred at the time of the interview. Ten percent switched their preference to another candidate, and 8 percent were undecideds who finally settled upon a candidate and voted. However, a plurality of swing voters, 33 percent, did not vote at all. That compares with 10 percent of committed voters who did not turn out. This propensity for swing voters not to participate is reduced significantly when other factors affecting the likelihood of voting are taken into account, but it does show that many swing voters are not voters at all.[6]

The 1996 postelection panel data tell a similar story—swing voters are much more likely to vote for their preferred candidate (36 percent) than to switch (8 percent) or to develop a preference (7 percent). But again, fully 42 percent of swing voters in the final preelection poll told Gallup that they did not vote, compared to 7 percent of committed voters.

In the 1996 panel, nonvoters were asked why they did not vote. Here, too, the responses of swing voters and committed voters differed. Twenty-nine percent of swing voters said they never bothered to register; 14 percent said

5. Because of the limited number of swing voters in the 2004 samples, these data are based on the responses from all respondents, without taking into account their registration status or likelihood to vote.

6. In 2004 there were a significant number whose actual behavior could not be ascertained because they refused to answer the basic voting question in either the pre- or postelection interview.

they did not vote because they did not like the candidates. Committed voters were most likely to mention work or family obligations as a reason for not voting (33 percent did), though a substantial proportion of swing voters (24 percent) also cited this reason. These results further underscore the notion that many swing voters are disengaged from the political process.

Conclusion

The long history of Gallup swing voter measurement points toward a number of significant conclusions:

1. It is difficult to get a precise estimate of the percentage of Americans who are swing voters. In particular, the number of swing voters varies depending on how questions designed to identify swing voters are worded. Swing voter estimates will also be lower if leaners are excluded from the definition. Finally, there will be fewer swing voters among the likely electorate (the likely voter group) than among the larger pool of registered voters and the full population of eligible voters.

2. Usually the percentage of swing voters declines over the course of a campaign, but that is not always the case. In 1988 and 1996, the proportion held fairly steady throughout, and in 1992 and, to a lesser extent, in 2000 it increased later in the campaign. Also, the dynamics of the campaign can greatly influence the percentage of swing voters, best exemplified by the effect of Perot's dropping out and reentering the race in 1992.

3. The "nonswing" or committed voters do not necessarily have immutable preferences. For example, the percentage of voters who were committed to George W. Bush in 2000 shrank as the campaign wore on. Obviously, some formerly committed Bush voters returned to being on the fence.

4. Because most supporters of third-party candidates entertain at least some thoughts of abandoning that candidate and voting for one of the major-party candidates, who have a better prospect of winning the election, a high-profile third-party candidate can increase the proportion of swing voters in a particular campaign. There were more swing voters in the 1992 and 1996 elections, when Perot received 19 and 8 percent of the vote, respectively, than in the more closely contested 2000 and 2004 elections, when all third-party candidates combined received less than 4 percent of the vote.

5. The percentage of swing voters has declined in each of the past two elections. This may be a reflection of a more polarized electorate, a trend that first became evident during the Clinton years and has become even more marked under Bush.

6. All of the swing voter questions have limitations, which is one reason why there have been changes over the years as to which question(s) were asked in a given campaign.

—The "any chance/no chance" wording, used between 1992 and 2004, tells where swing voters might go but does not give as precise an accounting of core support. A voter inclined to vote for the Democratic candidate who says that there is no chance he or she will vote for the Republican could still vote for an independent or minor-party candidate.

—The certain-to-vote wording has the opposite set of strengths and weaknesses—it gives a more precise measurement of core support but does not give information as to where swing voters might swing.

—The strength-of-support wording probably gives some sense of the voters' changeability but seems to be more a measure of the respondents' enthusiasm for their candidate.

7. Swing voters are not concentrated in a small number of demographic subgroups. In the three most recent presidential elections, there is no demographic group that is consistently and significantly over- or underrepresented among swing voters.

8. Swing voters do, however, have a number of distinctive attitudinal characteristics. When compared to more committed voters, swing voters are more likely to be independents and moderates and to be relatively disengaged from the political process.

9. On Election Day, most swing voters are likely to vote for whichever candidate they preferred, however weakly, before the election—or to stay home. Far fewer voters will switch to a different candidate or settle upon a candidate after being completely undecided.

Media attention on swing voters has increased greatly in the past twenty years. But the 2004 election may mark a shift in the way pundits approach swing voters. First, it was clear throughout the election that there were relatively few swing voters available. That may be a peculiarity of the 2004 election, or it may be a new reality in the era of a more politically polarized nation. Also, the Republicans' 2004 election strategy focused more on getting their loyalists to the polls, rather than trying to convince fence sitters to support them. Since that strategy proved successful, parties may try to devote more of their resources to activating their base than to wooing swing voters.

Even if campaigns reduce their efforts to persuade swing voters, this elusive American voter has become such a staple of election reporting that Gallup and other polling organizations will continue to monitor the swing vote in 2008 and beyond.

three
Campaign Dynamics and the Swing Vote in the 2004 Election

Michael Dimock, April Clark, and Juliana Menasce Horowitz

On November 2, 2004, over 122 million voters—60.3 percent of the American adult population—cast ballots for president after a long and tightly contested campaign.[1] How much that campaign mattered, however, depends on which voters one looks at. A nationwide survey conducted in the days after the election found that 61 percent of voters said they had made up their minds about whom to vote for before the parties had even held their nominating conventions in the summer, and well before the campaigns began in earnest.[2] Who, then, is the target of all the advertising, campaign speeches, organized debates, and other campaign efforts between August and November?

The answer, of course, is "swing voters"—but who these elusive voters are, whether they are really persuadable, and whether they will actually show up on Election Day are all important questions that have not yet been answered satisfactorily. In 2004, the Pew Research Center for the People and the Press undertook an extensive effort to measure and track the attitudes and behavior of swing voters throughout the campaign process. The results of the research suggest that swing voters are a significant factor in the course of a

---

1. See "2004 Voting-Age and Voting-Eligible Population Estimates and Voter Turnout," available at http://elections.gmu.edu/Voter_ Turnout_2004.htm.

2. Pew Research Center for the People and the Press, "Voters Liked Campaign 2004, but Too Much Mud-Slinging," Survey Report, November 11, 2004, available at www.people-press.org/reports/pdf/233.pdf.

presidential campaign. Though these voters are generally less engaged, the campaign helps them to learn about the candidates and to solidify their preferences. And though they turn out to vote at significantly lower rates than committed partisans, swing voters have the potential to be the decisive factor in any closely contested race.

Whether the campaign can serve to *change* the minds of swing voters, however, remains an open question. The results of two panel surveys that tracked the preferences of swing voters before and after the debates, and before and after the final weeks of the campaign, found that most swing voters expressed some candidate preference—however weak or uncertain— prior to these events, and that that preference was in most cases reinforced and strengthened, rather than challenged, by what these voters learned.

In this chapter, we summarize the results from a number of separate surveys conducted by the Pew Research Center during the summer and fall of 2004 to provide a broad overview of who the swing voters were, how they changed in the course of the campaign, and how they ended up voting on Election Day.

Campaign Effects and the Swing Voter

Since the first studies of voting behavior in the 1940s and 1950s, political scientists have debated whether campaigns really matter, and if so, for whom. From the seminal *Voting* (1954), by Bernard Berelson, Paul F. Lazarsfeld, and William N. McPhee, and *The American Voter* (1960), by Angus Campbell, Philip E. Converse, Warren E. Miller, and Donald E. Stokes, to more recent studies, many scholars have argued that voting decisions hinge on sociological and partisan identifications that exist before a campaign begins and that campaigns simply activate these latent preferences.[3] Since the 1990s, however, more studies have shown that campaigns do matter, although they may affect different voters differently.

Samuel Popkin and Thomas Holbrook both found that campaign events that disseminate information about candidates and issues to the public, such as party conventions and debates, play an important role in the voters' decisionmaking process.[4] Though many voters may not become fully informed about the candidates' policy platforms, voters utilize "information shortcuts"

---

3. Berelson, Lazarsfeld, and McPhee (1954); Campbell and others (1960). On the last point, see, for example, Bartels (1993).
4. Popkin (1991); Holbrook (1996).

or "heuristics" to draw meaningful inferences about the candidates that shape their voting decisions.

Further research has found that the information available during a campaign is especially helpful to voters at a medium level of information.[5] These are voters who are receptive to new information and who possess enough knowledge of public affairs to process what they learn in the course of a campaign. By comparison, campaign effects tend to be more muted for both voters who already possess a great deal of political knowledge and for those who know very little. Highly informed voters are often committed to partisan and ideological positions and are unlikely to be swayed by information revealed during a campaign, much of which will not be new to them. At the other end of the spectrum, voters who are disengaged from politics often lack the basic political knowledge needed to process the information they receive or pay so little attention to the campaign that they gain little help in deciding how to vote.

Swing voters, by definition, have not developed a committed preference for one of the candidates, but whether they can be persuaded by campaign events and communications may depend on where they fit in this spectrum. We will return to this question later in this chapter. First, however, a few definitions are in order.

Identifying the Swing Voters

The first step in identifying swing voters is operationalizing the concept into effective survey questions. The Pew Research Center employed a three-question series to identify those registered voters who were committed to one candidate, and those who were potentially open to persuasion. The first question asked respondents to identify their current presidential preference: "If the presidential election were being held today, would you vote for the Republican ticket of George W. Bush and Dick Cheney, the Democratic ticket of John Kerry and John Edwards, or the ticket of Ralph Nader and Peter Camejo?"[6]

Respondents who said they had not made up their minds or were unwilling to express a preference were probed with a second question in an effort to elicit whether or not they had any inclination at present: "As of *today*, do you *lean* more to . . . [same list of choices]?" These "leaners" were counted as

5. Hillygus and Jackman (2003); Zaller (1992).
6. To prevent possible order effects, the Republican and Democratic candidate response options were rotated. Unless otherwise indicated, all analyses in this chapter are based on registered voters.

Figure 3-1. Defining Swing Voters

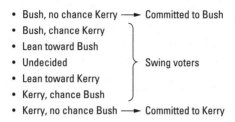

- Bush, no chance Kerry ——▶ Committed to Bush
- Bush, chance Kerry ⎤
- Lean toward Bush ⎟
- Undecided ⎬ Swing voters
- Lean toward Kerry ⎟
- Kerry, chance Bush ⎦
- Kerry, no chance Bush ——▶ Committed to Kerry

Source: Pew Research Center for the People and the Press.

swing voters because they lack a firm commitment to the candidate, but understanding their early impressions provides important information later as we track how the campaign influences their decisionmaking.

In addition to probing the undecideds, a third question was asked of those who did choose a candidate initially, in order to find out how committed they were to their choice. Bush supporters were asked, "Do you think there is a chance that you might vote for John Kerry in November, or have you definitely decided not to vote for him?" Kerry supporters received the same question about George W. Bush. On this basis, voters who said there was a chance they might change their minds by Election Day even though they did have a current preference were counted as swing voters.

The distinction between swing and nonswing voters rests on the responses provided to these three items. In effect, the questions allowed us to divide the electorate into seven groups, ranging from the most committed Bush supporters to the most committed Kerry supporters. All five groups in between were classified as "swing voters" (see figure 3-1). For analytical purposes, "committed" voters were individuals who indicated a preference for Bush or Kerry and had no intention of changing their minds. Swing voters consist of individuals who failed to provide any vote preference, said they were leaning toward Bush or Kerry but had not yet made up their minds, or said they favored a candidate but there was still a chance they would vote for the other candidate.[7]

As with any operationalization, the fit between the measure and any individual's actual status may not be perfect. Some respondents may insist that they will never switch but in the end do. Others may claim to be uncommit-

7. A small group of respondents expressed a preference for Ralph Nader in 2004 pre-election surveys, but there were too few to analyze separately, and they are removed from the analysis here.

ted, when in fact—whether consciously or unconsciously—they have already made up their minds. These concerns are important, but they are largely unavoidable in the survey context. Our operating rule here is to take people at their word. If they tell us they like one candidate but there is a chance they might still vote for another, they are classified as a swing voter.

In 2004, the number of voters who fell into the swing voter category by this method ranged from 28 percent of registered voters in the period before the conventions to just 19 percent on the eve of the election. The size and shifting preferences of swing voters will be discussed later in the chapter, but first it is valuable to look at how they differ from committed voters.

Who Are the Swing Voters?

At any point during the campaign, swing voters make up only a minority of the eligible electorate, and a demographic profile of swing voters shows some key characteristics that set them apart from the majority who have more committed preferences. To evaluate these differences in detail, four surveys conducted between September and October are combined in table 3-1 to provide a substantial base on which to make comparisons.[8]

Swing voters as a group have less education and lower incomes than do voters who are committed to a presidential candidate. A 51 percent majority of swing voters never attended college, compared with 42 percent of committed voters. But in other respects, the profile of swing voters matches the profile of committed voters quite closely. In terms of age, gender, race, and ethnicity, swing voters differ at most only slightly from their more decisive counterparts.

The other two columns in table 3-1 provide similar demographic data on committed Bush and Kerry voters. In many respects, the 2004 swing voters were more likely to resemble Kerry's committed supporters than voters who were supporting Bush. Women made up the majority of both swing and committed Kerry voters (56 percent each), whereas the majority of committed Bush voters (52 percent) were male. Thirty-five percent of swing voters and 34 percent of Kerry supporters reported annual incomes of less than $30,000, compared with 21 percent of committed Bush supporters. Similarly,

---

8. Even though the swing voter group changes in size over the course of the campaign, an analysis of the demographic characteristics of swing voters throughout this period finds little variation, allowing us to merge data from multiple points in time for illustrative purposes.

Table 3-1. Demographic Characteristics of Swing and Committed Voters[a]

Percent

	Swing voters	Committed voters	Committed to Bush	Committed to Kerry
Percentage of registered voters	21	79	40	39
Gender				
Male	44	48	52	44
Female	56	52	48	56
Age				
18–29	19	17	15	18
30–49	38	39	42	37
50–64	23	26	26	26
Over 65	20	18	17	19
Race and ethnicity				
White	77	80	90	70
Black	12	11	2	20
Hispanic (any race)	11	9	8	10
Family income				
Less than $20,000	21	15	11	20
$20,000 to $29,999	14	12	10	14
$30,000 to $49,999	25	26	26	26
$50,000 to $74,999	16	18	20	15
$75,000 to $99,999	11	14	16	11
$100,000 or more	13	15	17	14
Education				
High school graduate or less	51	42	40	43
Some college or technical	24	27	29	24
College graduate	17	19	20	19
Post-graduate	8	12	11	14
N	1,319	5,344	2,802	2,542

Source: Pew Research Center for the People and the Press.

a. Based on registered voters from four surveys conducted prior to the 2004 election (September 8–14, October 1–3, October 15–19, and October 27–30).

just 77 percent of swing voters and 70 percent of Kerry voters were white, versus 90 percent of Bush backers.

Swing voters also differ from committed voters in political orientation (see table 3-2). The majority of swing voters do not think of themselves as partisans—just 43 percent identify themselves as Democrats or Republicans, compared with nearly three-quarters (74 percent) of voters who are committed to one or the other candidate and two thirds (67 percent) of registered voters overall. Similarly, swing voters tend to think of themselves as "middle of the road" ideologically, if they even consider ideological labels at all. A 53 percent majority of swing voters either describe themselves as moderates or say they don't know where they fit, in ideological terms. This is in stark contrast to the

Table 3-2. Party and Ideology of Swing and Committed Voters[a]
Percent

	All voters	Committed voters	Swing voters
Party			
Republican	33	37	19
Democrat	34	37	24
Independent	27	23	40
No preference	3	2	6
Other/don't know	3	1	11
Ideology			
Conservative	41	43	32
Liberal	17	18	15
Moderate	37	36	43
Don't know	5	3	10
N	6,663	5,344	1,319

Source: Pew Research Center for the People and the Press.
a. Based on registered voters in four surveys conducted prior to the 2004 election (September 8–14; October 1–3; October 15–19; and October 27–30).

61 percent of committed voters who describe themselves as either liberal or conservative.

Younger voters typically have far weaker partisan preferences than their elders, and swing voters, too, are less likely to identify with one of the two major parties; so it is a striking finding that there are no significant age differences between swing voters and committed voters (see table 3-1). Just 19 percent of swing voters are under age thirty, a proportion comparable to the number found among voters committed to Kerry and Bush. Despite a greater propensity to think of themselves as political independents, younger voters (age eighteen to forty-nine) develop firm candidate preferences at about the same rate as their more senior counterparts.

Campaign Attentiveness

Swing voters are substantially less enthusiastic about politics and public affairs than voters who have stronger candidate preferences. Just half say they follow government and public affairs most of the time, compared with 64 percent of committed voters. This lack of engagement is linked to the propensity, or lack of it, to vote. Just 53 percent of swing voters say that they "always vote," well below the 62 percent of more committed voters who describe themselves this way.

Swing voters are also considerably less likely to be knowledgeable about the candidates. In late October, two weeks before Election Day, survey respondents were asked to identify two basic platform elements that were central to the campaign—which candidate favored allowing workers to invest some of their Social Security contributions in the stock market (Bush) and which candidate favored federal funding of medical research using stem cells from human embryos (Kerry). Just 34 percent of swing voters could answer these two questions correctly, compared with 48 percent of those committed to a candidate.

Yet despite being less engaged in politics and not as able as committed voters to identify key elements of the major candidates' platforms, swing voters are often the targets of political advertising and are courted heavily by campaigns, especially in a close election. If campaigns influence voters by delivering information, how attentive swing voters are to the campaign is a critical factor.

Swing voters may be characterized as a middle-awareness group.[9] They do not follow the campaign as closely and do not give as much thought to the election as voters who make up their minds in the early stages of the campaign, but they are not as disengaged as those who are not registered voters. In August of 2004, before the campaign was in full swing, about two-thirds of swing voters said they were following news about the presidential campaign very closely or fairly closely. Among committed voters, 80 percent were following the campaign very closely or fairly closely at this early stage, whereas among those who were not registered to vote, only 55 percent reported following the campaign this closely.

Campaign interest is a dynamic phenomenon, typically increasing as Election Day nears. This trend is particularly noticeable among swing voters. Figure 3-2 tracks how much thought the public gave to the election during the last four months of the campaign. In July, about half of swing voters had given a lot of thought to the presidential election, compared with 73 percent of voters who had already made up their minds and 38 percent of those who were not registered to vote. As the campaign progressed, swing voters became increasingly attentive to the election, with two-thirds saying they had given a lot of thought to the campaign by the weekend before Election Day. Throughout this period, swing voters remained positioned between committed voters and nonvoters when evaluated in terms of how much thought they had given to the election.

9. Zaller (1992).

Figure 3-2. Voters Who Have Thought "a Lot" about the 2004 Presidential Election

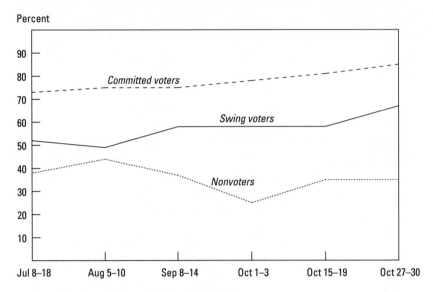

Source: Pew Research Center for the People and the Press.

Overall Trends in Swing Voter Movement

Consistent with the literature on political attentiveness and campaign effects, swing voters should be well positioned to process information received during the campaign and to move into the committed camp as they learn more about the candidates. This expectation was borne out in the summer of 2004. Following the Democratic National Convention, July 26 to 29, when the challenger John Kerry established the basic themes of his campaign and introduced himself to a broader pool of voters than had followed the primaries, the number of swing voters fell from 28 percent of the electorate to 22 percent (see figure 3-3). Interestingly, while the number of committed Kerry voters rose 3 percentage points following the Democratic National Convention, so did committed support for Bush. In the survey conducted immediately after the Republican National Convention, August 30 to September 2, the number of swing voters did not change substantially, perhaps because most Americans were already familiar with George W. Bush.

There is also evidence that swing voters used the information disseminated during the debate period to help resolve their uncertainties. Debates are among the most visible campaign activities, and even voters who do not watch the

Figure 3-3. Swing and Committed Voters as a Percentage of Registered Voters, 2004

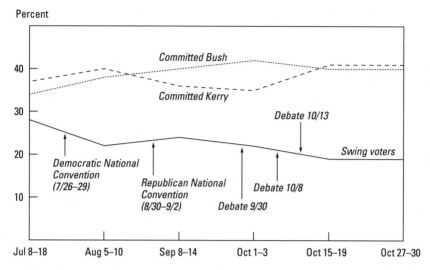

Source: Pew Research Center for the People and the Press.

debates are likely to learn about the performance of the candidates through media coverage of the event.[10] The 2004 presidential debates appear to have helped a number of voters solidify their candidate preferences. Prior to the first debate, 24 percent of registered voters were in the swing voter category. By the end of the four debates (three presidential and one vice-presidential), the swing vote reached its lowest level of the campaign, with fewer than one-fifth of registered voters still failing to make a firm commitment to a candidate by mid- to late October.

Arriving at a Decision

Tracking the relative size of the swing vote over time provides some insight into aggregate dynamics, but it cannot answer what is perhaps the key question: Can we predict how swing voters will end up voting? For this, our research needed to follow individual swing voters over time, to see how the campaign changed their attitudes toward the candidates. To accomplish this goal, the Pew Research Center conducted two panel surveys. The first of these was aimed at understanding the impact of the debates and thus involved recontacting in

10. Holbrook (1999); Shaw (1999).

Table 3-3. Changes in Voter Commitment in the September-to-October Callback Study[a]
Percent

October callback	September preference		
	Committed to Bush	Swing voters	Committed to Kerry
Committed to Bush	95	22	1
Swing voters	5	51	5
Committed to Kerry	*	27	94

Source: Pew Research Center for the People and the Press.
a. Figures are based on 1,001 registered voters from three surveys conducted September 8–14, September 17–21, and September 22–26, who were re-interviewed in a callback poll, October 21–25, 2004.
* Less than .5 percent.

October, after the final debate, respondents originally reached in September, when the number of swing voters was high. The second panel first contacted voters in early to mid-October and then recontacted them immediately after Election Day to find out how they voted. The results of these panel studies are consistent with the overall trends seen in our regular polling—the number of swing voters fell significantly after the debates, with more attentive swing voters considerably more likely to commit to a candidate than those who were less engaged. However, the results take us an important step further in revealing the direction swing voters shifted as they learned from the campaign.

Combining the results from several surveys, 26 percent of the electorate were classified as swing voters in surveys conducted during September, following the Democratic and Republican conventions but prior to the first presidential debate. But when reached again by phone in mid-October, just 17 percent of these same respondents remained in this category. Put another way, nearly one in ten voters reached a firm commitment during the debate period, moving from the "swing" to the "committed" category.

Notably, neither Bush nor Kerry gained a significant advantage from this shift—the number of committed supporters of each candidate grew by almost equal amounts. Table 3-3 reveals why this was the case. Of those who said they were certain about their preference in September, 95 percent stuck with that preference after the debates were finished. However, nearly half of the swing voters (49 percent) moved from the swing to the committed category. But neither candidate gained much from this shift—22 percent of swing voters moved to being committed Bush supporters, while 27 percent became committed Kerry supporters.

The callback design allows us to look more closely at those early swing voters who made up their minds during the debate period, and the results

Table 3-4. Views about the Election of Swing Voters in September 2004[a]

Percent

	All voters	Committed throughout campaign	Now decided	Still swing voters
Amount of thought given to election				
A lot	81	85	77	64
Little	15	11	17	30
Some/don't know	4	4	6	6
Does it matter who wins the election?				
Yes	77	83	71	53
No	19	14	24	39
Don't know	4	3	5	8
Did you watch the presidential debates?				
Yes, watched	82	85	79	71
Watched a lot or all	46	50	43	30
Watched some	24	23	25	27
Watched a little	12	12	11	14
No, didn't watch	18	15	21	29
Don't know	*	0	0	*
N	1,001	482	269	250

Source: Pew Research Center for the People and the Press.

a. Figures are based on 1,001 registered voters from three surveys conducted September 8–14, September 17–21, and September 22–26, who were re-interviewed in a callback poll, October 21–25, 2004.

* Less than .5 percent.

confirm that attentiveness is a significant factor separating the committed from the swing voters (see table 3-4). In the postdebate survey, fully 85 percent of voters who were committed to a candidate throughout the study said they had given a lot of thought to the election, compared with just 64 percent of swing voters who still had not made up their minds. Those who had been swing voters in September but had now decided fell, not surprisingly, somewhere in the middle—77 percent had given a lot of thought to the campaign.

The increased attention given to the campaign appears to be part of what helped these newly decided voters make up their minds—and by October they looked more like the voters who had decided early on than like those who were still undecided or only weakly committed. Forty-three percent said they watched either all or a lot of the presidential debates, compared with 50 percent of early committers, but far more than the 30 percent of voters who were still uncommitted. They also cared more about the election outcome—71 percent of newly decided voters said that it really mattered who won the election, well above the 53 percent among those who had not yet made up their minds.

Table 3-5. Relationship Between September and October Voter Preferences
Percent

October callback	September preference				
	Committed to Bush	Favor Bush	Undecided	Favor Kerry	Committed to Kerry
Committed to Bush	95	44	14	12	1
Favor Bush	2	28	11	11	0
Undecided	1	7	36	7	2
Favor Kerry	2	10	13	16	3
Committed to Kerry	*	8	23	53	94
N	241	159	145	130	239

Source: Pew Research Center for the People and the Press.
* Less than .5 percent.

To further unpack what happened to swing voters, table 3-5 breaks the swing voters out into three subcategories: those who had a weak preference for Bush in September, those who had a weak preference for Kerry, and those who were completely undecided. The results show that swing voters who had expressed at least a weak preference in September were far more likely to be moved by the debates than the undecideds. Of those who initially favored Kerry, 65 percent had committed to a candidate by mid-October, as had 52 percent of those who initially favored Bush. But among the undecideds, just 37 percent had committed to either Bush or Kerry by mid-October, while an equal number (36 percent) remained undecided.

Not only can we see that many voters made up their minds during the debate period, but we can see in which direction they moved, and the results confirm expectations. By a margin of 53 percent to 12 percent, most voters who favored Kerry ended up becoming committed Kerry supporters rather than Bush supporters after the debates. Similarly, the debates reinforced the early leanings of those who favored Bush—44 percent were committed to Bush by mid-October whereas just 8 percent had become committed Kerry supporters.

In short, the evidence supports two key hypotheses about how campaign information is likely to influence swing voters: campaign effects are more noticeable among more engaged voters; and campaigns tend to reinforce, rather than challenge, prior leanings. This latter point is particularly important with respect to the impact of presidential debates. Although pundits and overnight polls often deliver a quick judgment as to who won or lost in a debate, the real judgment is in the eye of the beholder. Swing voters with a

Table 3-6. Changes in Voter Preferences in the October-to-November Callback Study[a]

Percent

November vote choice	October Preference		
	Committed to Bush	Committed to Kerry	Swing voters
Bush	96	1	35
Kerry	1	97	43
Nader	*	0	*
Other	*	1	5
Refused to answer	3	1	16
N	535	462	197

Source: Pew Research Center for the People and the Press.

a. Figures are based on 1,209 registered voters from two surveys conducted October 1–3 and October 15–19, who were re-interviewed in a November callback poll, November 5–8, 2004.

* Less than .5 percent.

leaning toward Bush or Kerry are far more likely to see evidence that reinforces their initial leaning than to register information that counters their prior beliefs.

The second Pew panel study, conducted after the election, recontacted individuals who had originally been interviewed in early to mid-October to find out how they ultimately voted. Once again, the results, shown in table 3-6, confirm that respondents who express a firm commitment to their candidate—those who say there is no chance they will change their mind—are in fact unlikely to be shaken from their position. Virtually all voters in these categories ended up voting for the candidate they expected to. The outcome among voters who were still uncommitted in October was divided: 35 percent ended up voting for Bush, and 43 percent voted for Kerry (16 percent refused to say whom they had voted for). This advantage for Kerry is consistent with the overall trend in the late polls, which showed Kerry closing the gap on a slim Bush lead in the last week of the campaign. Unfortunately, because the survey had only a limited number of cases, we cannot confirm a statistically significant advantage for Kerry among late-deciding swing voters, nor can we break these late swing voters into subgroups for a more detailed analysis.

How Swing Voters View the Campaign

Even after the campaign was over, voters who had more difficulty making up their minds stood apart in how they viewed the campaign (see table 3-7). Classifying voters in the postelection callback study by their status in October

Table 3-7. Views of the 2004 Campaign by Swing and Committed Voters[a]

Percent

	Status in October		
	All voters	Committed voters	Swing voters[b]
Satisfaction with choice of candidates			
Very satisfied	33	37	17
Fairly satisfied	33	31	40
Not very satisfied	16	14	21
Not at all satisfied	16	16	20
Don't know	2	2	2
My vote was . . .			
For my candidate	60	62	48
Against the opponent	34	33	43
Don't know	6	5	9
Learned enough to make a choice?			
Yes, learned enough	86	88	74
No, did not learn enough	13	11	24
Don't know	1	1	2
I found the presidential debates . . .			
Helpful	62	61	65
Not helpful	33	34	28
Did not watch	4	4	6
Don't know	1	1	1
N	1,209	997	207

Source: Pew Research Center for the People and the Press.

a. Figures are based on 1,209 registered voters from two surveys conducted October 1–3 and October 15–19, who were re-interviewed in a November callback poll, November 5–8, 2004.

b. Respondents still not committed to a candidate in the October polls.

reveals that swing voters took a generally more negative view of the campaign. Just 17 percent of those still swinging in October said that they were very satisfied with the choice of candidates, compared with 37 percent of those who had made up their minds before that point. As a result, only 48 percent of October swing voters said they voted *for* their preferred candidate, whereas 43 percent said they were primarily voting *against* his opponent. By contrast, 62 percent of committed Bush and Kerry voters voted *for* their candidate and only 33 percent voted *against* his opponent. The survey also shows that by November, 88 percent of committed voters felt they had learned enough about the candidates and issues to make an informed choice, whereas only 74 percent of swing voters voiced that sentiment. The presidential debates, however, stand out as an important factor for both committed and swing voters. The two groups were equally likely to say that the debates were helpful to them in making up their minds.

Conclusion

Our investigation of swing voters in the 2004 election cycle confirms a number of expectations. We find that the number of swing voters tends to decrease as voters learn from the election campaign, that campaign events tend to reinforce prior leanings among voters who express a preference early on, and that campaign effects appear to be greatest for voters in the middle range of political attentiveness.

The evidence that most swing voters in 2004 gravitated toward their initial leaning raises a critical question about whether swing voters are a meaningful group to analyze at all. Perhaps, while professing an openness to consider other candidates, many of these swing voters were in reality just as committed to their choices early on as those we have labeled committed voters. Yet this study has also provided considerable evidence that swing voters are more influenced by the campaign than committed voters. Table 3-5, in particular, shows that during the period of the presidential debates, committed voters behaved just as they had said they would: 95 percent stayed with their preferred candidate, while almost none of them became supporters, committed or otherwise, of the other candidate. By contrast, those swing voters who had a preferred candidate but were not firmly committed to him were, as promised, much more variable. About 50 percent became firm supporters of their initial favorite—but 20 percent switched camps entirely. Finally, those who insisted they were completely undecided split about evenly into three groups: 36 percent stayed undecided, 36 percent became firm or weak Kerry supporters, and 25 percent swung toward Bush. In short, swing voters are more influenced by campaign events because many enter the campaign without having focused on the choice they face. The fact that swing voters have given less consideration to the campaign and have less information about the candidates means that the new information that they do acquire has a greater impact on these voters. And while campaign information appears to mostly reinforce these voters' prior preferences, this is not always the case.

It is undoubtedly the case that some of those classified as swing voters are actually less open to persuasion than they say (or think) they are; nevertheless, this study confirms that many voters do not form clear candidate preferences until late in the election cycle and that these voters are deeply affected by what they learn during the campaign. No survey questionnaire will ever successfully divide the decided from the persuadable with perfect accuracy, because many respondents do not themselves know their own minds. But in close races, identifying swing voters provides a critical analytical tool for understanding how campaign events are influencing the direction of the race.

References

Bartels, Larry. 1993. "Messages Received: The Political Impact of Media Exposure." *American Political Science Review* 87: 267–85.

Berelson, Bernard R., Paul F. Lazarsfeld, and William N. McPhee. 1954. *Voting: A Study of Opinion Formation in a Presidential Campaign.* University of Chicago Press.

Campbell, Angus, Philip E. Converse, Warren E. Miller, and Donald E. Stokes. 1960. *The American Voter.* New York: Wiley.

Hillygus, D. Sunshine, and Simon Jackman. 2003. "Voter Decision Making in Election 2000: Campaign Effect, Partisan Activation, and the Clinton Legacy." *American Journal of Political Science* 47: 583–96.

———. 1996. *Do Campaigns Matter?* Thousand Oaks, Calif.: Sage Publications.

Holbrook, Thomas M. 1999. "Political Learning from Presidential Debates." *Political Behavior* 21: 67–89.

Popkin, Samuel L. 1994. *The Reasoning Voter: Communication and Persuasion in Presidential Campaigns.* 2nd ed. University of Chicago Press.

Shaw, Daron R. 1999. "A Study of Presidential Campaign Event Effects from 1952 to 1992." *Journal of Politics* 61: 387–422.

Zaller, John R. 1992. *The Nature and Origins of Mass Opinion.* Cambridge University Press.

four
Swing Voting and
U.S. Presidential Elections

Daron R. Shaw

As American national elections have become more competitive, political consultants and the news media have shifted their attention away from reliable partisans and toward voters whose preferences might be influenced by the campaign. As a result, every election since 1990 has seen one or more groups proffered up as a "swing" group whose vote decision will determine the election. Reagan Democrats, Latinos, soccer moms, NASCAR dads, Catholics, and rural voters have all had their day in the sun. Similarly, small groups of swing voters are interviewed and probed on national television by consultants such as Frank Luntz or reporters such as Judy Woodruff for clues about what will happen on Election Day.

This makes for entertaining television viewing and newspaper reading, but there are obvious deficiencies in the popular understanding of swing voting. More specifically, there is no common definition or metric for measuring swing voting or swing groups. This means that the news media parrot the sometimes banal and often ill-defined demographic explanations offered by political consulting companies. This is particularly troublesome in the case of swing voting because it is unclear whether there is any coherent sociology or group basis to swing voting. It may be that swing voting is driven by psychological attributes that are scattered across any and all politically relevant groups. This raises the very real possibility that campaigns and the news media are seriously off track in their efforts to sensibly interpret voting dynamics.

In this chapter, I take aim at swing voting. My central arguments are straightforward. First, I contend that swing voting is distinct from any number of concepts that are often (and erroneously) used as surrogates for swing voting. Second, I argue that while swing voting was common and important in the 2000 and 2004 presidential elections, it seems to have declined since the period from 1968 to 1976. Third, I believe individual psychological factors are significantly more important for explaining swing voting than being a member of a particular group.

I proceed by first examining the notion that swing voters are those who claim to be undecided in public opinion surveys of presidential election preferences. This approach has led many to believe that incumbents are at a disadvantage in an election in which there are many swing voters, and that swing voting is rooted in group identities. I consider a variety of presidential polling and voting data from 1948 to 2004, much of which calls into question the equation of indecision and swing voting. I then examine the usefulness and accuracy of the swing groups bandied about by practitioners and the news media in 2000 and 2004. In so doing, I compare two heretofore distinct variable sets—political demography and psychological engagement—to explain presidential voter volatility. My empirical analyses draw on panel data from the American National Election Studies (ANES) to estimate the relative frequency of presidential swing voting from 1968 to 1976 and from 1996 to 2004 and to test the effects of an array of potential correlates. The results demonstrate that more than one-quarter of Americans are swing voters and that psychological factors dominate other explanations for the relative propensity of voters to be persuaded by a given presidential election campaign.

What the Classics Say about Swing Voting

The idea that certain voters are more likely to be persuadable than others is not new. The Columbia studies, especially *Voting* and *The People's Choice*, note this in their panel data from Erie County, Ohio, and Elmira, New York, arguing that voters who are "cross-pressured" by their group identities and social networks are the most likely to either abstain from voting or have variable preferences.[1] The Michigan school, exemplified by *The American Voter*, offers a slightly different perspective, suggesting that voters with heterogeneous social contexts are more likely to develop conflicting attitudinal predispositions and,

---

1. Berelson, Lazarsfeld, and McPhee (1954); Lazarsfeld, Berelson, and Gaudet (1948).

therefore, variable vote preferences.[2] Then there are rational-choice models of mass behavior, which posit that voters near the median of the ideological spectrum are swing voters; if candidates behave rationally,[3] they will target their messages at voters at or near the median, presenting these voters with a difficult decision calculus, which in turn should produce ambiguity toward the candidates and volatility in voters' preferences.[4]

In considering these seminal studies, however, we see the core problem. There is little specific, acknowledged connective tissue between the different concepts advanced by political science, or between these and the layperson's notion of swing voters. For the layperson, a commonsense definition of swing voting would be voters whose candidate preferences tend to be variable, and whose ultimate decisions will determine the outcome of the election. Campaign professionals incorporate this conception into their methodologies for identifying swing counties and precincts; they define swing voting as the difference between the high and low vote percentages for a party across some number of recent elections.[5] But political science has committed to neither a single term nor a common definition for this phenomenon. This leaves us to compare apples with oranges and highlights the need for clarification and extension.

Conceptions of Swing Voting in the News Media

In the absence of any strong, consistent definition or understanding of swing voting, those who make their living in politics, including members of the media, have relied on practical surrogates and descriptive measures. First and foremost, many in the news media equate swing voting with lack of commitment to one of the candidates. That is, reporters and pundits believe that anyone who says she does not know for whom she is voting is a swing voter. A second, attendant development is that the news media often seek to identify

2. Campbell and others (1960).
3. Behaving rationally is defined as seeking to realize one's preference, which is (in this case) winning the election.
4. Downs (1957).
5. Shea and Burton (2003). This definition was articulated in *The Hotline*, a daily political on-line newsletter and staple for Beltway politicos: "The relative volatility of the electorate is known as the 'swing factor'—a statistical measure used in order to determine where and with which sub-group the race is unpredictable. From that, the term 'swing voters' was coined" (http://nationaljournal.com/about/hotline [December 10, 1999]). Thus, the swing voting rate in a given constituency i across elections t to $t + 5$ can be defined as follows:

Swing Voting Rate $^{i, t, \ldots, t+5}$ =

(maximum Democratic vote percentage) − (minimum Democratic vote percentage).

broad, demographically coherent groups as "swing" groups. Because news coverage focuses much of its attention on the attitudes and behavior of these individuals—for example, focus groups of "undecided voters" were convened by CNN, MSNBC, and ABC News during the 2000 and 2004 elections—the fundamental equation of swing voting with "undecided" respondents in surveys and the accuracy of group-based conceptions of swing voters is worth examining in some detail. Let us begin with the notion that undecided voters are swing voters.

After sifting through news and popular accounts of the 2000 and 2004 presidential elections, two common beliefs about undecided voters stand out. First, almost everyone agrees that there were few undecided voters in these elections: when we look at all available national polls, on average 6 percent of registered voters were undecided in April 2004 compared to 12 percent in April 1996 and April 2000 and 15 percent in April 1992. This comports with the common belief that the electorate was polarized in 2004, and that swing voters are something of an endangered species. It is also one of the reasons that reporters and pundits turned their attention away from swing voters to turnout and mobilization in 2004.

This "fact," however, is something of a methodological artifact. The percentage of undecided voters in a sample depends on both the actual incidence of "indecision" and the methodology of the pollster. For example, pollsters who ask a straight vote-choice question ("If the election were held tomorrow, would you vote for George W. Bush, John Kerry, or haven't you made up your mind?"), without mentioning the partisanship of the candidates or pushing undecided respondents to say which candidate they "lean" toward, will get a relatively higher percentage of undecided voters than pollsters who do include such items in their questions. Furthermore, the norm for preelection polls (and certainly those immediately prior to the election) is to push voters to declare a vote choice.

As we compare the percentage of "undecided" voters from year to year, one way to take into account this tendency to "push" voters into declaring a preference is to hold the polling organization constant. A cursory glance at the Gallup Poll's October surveys from recent presidential elections suggests that voters in 2004 were more likely to have a candidate preference than they were in 1992 and 1996, although the differences are small.[6] There is, in short, little reason to think undecided voters were any more endangered in 2000 or 2004 than they have been in other recent presidential elections.

6. See, for example, Wlezien and Erikson (2002).

Another common belief—especially in 2004—is that undecided voters (read, "swing voters") break for the challenger. This belief is part of the received wisdom of political consultants, who draw on experiences in legislative races. The underlying logic is simple: elections are referenda on the incumbent, and those who are ambivalent about backing the incumbent during the fall campaign usually vote for the challenger on Election Day.[7]

This notion is consistent with some of the literature in political psychology and has empirical backing. In 1989, Nick Panagakis analyzed results from 155 surveys, most from the late 1980s, that were conducted during the last week before an election. He found that in 82 percent of the cases, undecideds "broke" for the challenger. Panagakis concludes:

> Incumbent races should not be characterized in terms of point spread. [Suppose] a poll shows one candidate leading 50 percent to 40 percent, with 10 percent undecided. . . . Since most of the 10 points in the undecided category are likely to go to the challenger, polls are a lot closer than they look—50 percent to 40 percent is likely to become 52 percent to 48 percent, on election day.[8]

In 2004, Chris Bowers found that although there are some signs that the incumbent rule—that the incumbent rarely gets a higher vote percentage on Election Day than he or she polls beforehand—might be weakening in state and local races, it has even stronger support in presidential elections. In twenty-eight surveys involving presidential elections, Bowers claims, 86 percent show undecideds breaking mostly to the challenger.[9] Similarly, Guy Molyneaux averaged "the final surveys conducted by the three major networks and their partners" in the last four presidential elections featuring an incumbent and found:

> In three of these the incumbent fell short of or merely matched his final poll number, while exceeding it only once, and then by just a single point (Ronald Reagan). On average, the incumbent comes in half a point below his final poll result. . . . In every case, the challenger(s)—I include Ross Perot in 1992 and 1996—exceed their final poll result by at least 2 points, and the average gain is 4 points. In

---

7. See Chris Bowers, "Incumbent Rule Research Update," www.mydd.com/story/2004/9/3/22294/96534 (2004); Guy Molyneaux, "The Big Five-Oh," www.prospect.org/cs/articles?articleId=8694 (2004); and Panagakis (1989).

8. Panagakis (1989).

9. Bowers, "Incumbent Rule Research Update."

Figure 4-1. Final Gallup Poll Presidential Vote Projections, as Compared to the Actual Results[a]

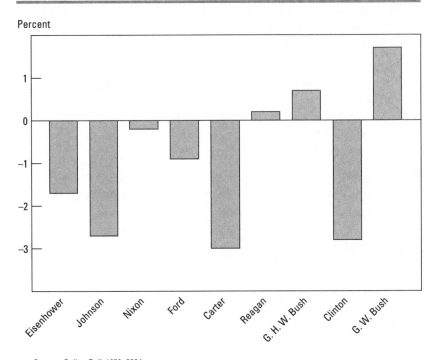

Percent

Source: Gallup Poll, 1956–2004.

a. Bars indicate how much greater or smaller the final Gallup Poll prediction of the incumbent president's share of the popular vote was compared to the actual result.

1980, Ronald Reagan received 51 percent, fully 6 percentage points above his final poll results.[10]

Finally, Mark Blumenthal, writing in 2004 (see figure 4-1; 2004 data added to figure), points out an intriguing pattern in the Gallup Poll's final vote projections:

> In the presidential elections since 1956 that featured an incumbent, the final projection of the incumbent's vote *exceeded* the incumbent's actual vote six of eight times. . . . On average, Gallup's projection of the incumbent's vote has averaged 1.3 percentage points greater than the actual result. Obviously, without seeing the raw results we can only

10. Molyneaux, "Big Five-Oh."

Table 4-1. How Undecideds Voted, 1948–2004[a]

Percent

Presidential election	Voted for challenger party	Voted for incumbent party	Voted other	Didn't vote
1948	22	44	1	33
1952	49	38	0	13
1956	29	52	1	18
1960	51	33	2	14
1964	48	39	2	11
1968	33	42	9	16
1972	52	29	1	17
1976	40	33	3	23
1980	42	27	11	24
1984	37	38	2	24
1988	44	27	1	28
1992	24	27	31	18
1996	31	31	16	22
2000	46	29	5	20
2004	18	25	0	57
Average of all elections	38	34	6	23
Average when incumbent presidents run for reelection	34	35	7	25

Source: American National Election Studies pre- and postelection surveys.

a. Preelection interviewing occurred from early September through the day before the election. Postelection interviews occurred in November, after the election.

speculate, but this pattern suggests that Gallup has allocated too many of the undecided over the years to incumbents.[11]

Should we therefore assume that undecided voters (and, by extension, swing voters) break heavily for the challenger in presidential elections? Although the preliminary data supporting this conclusion are formidable, I think there are strong reasons to be skeptical of the conventional wisdom. First, the dominant characteristic of undecided voters (however ascertained) is not their party identification or demographic profile. It is, rather, their tendency to be less interested, less involved, and less politically motivated. They are disproportionately likely to stay at home on Election Day. The data in table 4-1, taken from ANES surveys from 1948 to 2000, show that almost one-fourth of undecided voters do not vote.

11. Mark Blumenthal, "Do Undecided Voters Break for the Challenger?" www.mystery pollster.com/main/2004/09/do_undecided_vo.html (2004).

Second, despite the analyses cited earlier, the received wisdom about undecided voters breaking for the challenger has not been systematically analyzed for presidential elections, where information (especially about the challenger) is more readily available. The most reliable data set available to study individual voters is the ANES, which interviews people in September and October of an election year and then re-interviews them immediately after the election. Going back to 1948, table 4-1 shows how undecided voters (as determined by their responses in the preelection survey) ended up voting. Overall, it is clear that undecided voters do *not* break decisively one way or the other. The overall average is 38 percent for the challenger, 34 percent for the incumbent party candidate, 6 percent for third-party candidates, and 23 percent not voting. For years in which an incumbent president was running for reelection, the averages are 34 percent for the challenger, 35 percent for the incumbent, and 7 percent for third-party candidates.[12] With 25 percent not voting, this indicates that one would need either a huge pool of undecided voters or an anomalous outcome for undecided voters' decisions to sway the total vote more than 1 percentage point.

Having said this, it is true that undecided voters tend to break disproportionately for the candidate who turns out to be the *winner* in close races. Moreover, in five of these eight close presidential races, undecideds broke for the out-party's candidate: Eisenhower in 1952, Kennedy in 1960, Carter in 1976, Reagan in 1980, and Bush in 2000. The anomalous years are 1948, 1968, and 2004, when undecided voters went for Truman, Humphrey, and Bush, respectively.

The flip side of this is that undecideds break evenly or slightly for the underdog in blowout races. For example, they broke for Goldwater in 1964 and McGovern in 1972, while splitting in 1984 and 1996. The dynamic appears to be that wavering partisans come home after flirting with the out-party's winning candidate.

Of course, this analysis does not consider that some of the undecided voter pool includes respondents who were interviewed in early September. These people may have made up their minds shortly thereafter, rather than in the last few days of the campaign. Table 4-2 focuses squarely on voters who say they decided in the last two weeks of the campaign. From 1948 to 2004, an average of 47 percent of late deciders voted for the challenger, while 45 per-

---

12. The tendency of undecideds to vote for the incumbent is slightly overstated with the inclusion of the 1956 and 1948 elections, in which these voters broke for Eisenhower and Truman, respectively.

Table 4-2. How Late Deciders Voted, 1948–2004[a]

Percent

Election year	Voted for challenger party	Voted for incumbent party	Voted other
1948	14	83	3
1952	64	36	0
1956	32	67	1
1960	70	27	3
1964	54	46	0
1968	49	43	8
1972	68	29	3
1976	54	42	4
1980	56	29	15
1984	47	50	3
1988	47	50	3
1992	35	29	36
1996	33	42	25
2000	40	55	5
2004	38	53	0
Average	47	45	7
Average when incumbent presidents run for reelection	42	48	10

Source: American National Election Studies pre- and postelection surveys.
a. "Late deciders" are those who say they decided on their vote in the last week or on Election Day.

cent voted for the incumbent-party candidate. Focusing only on races with an incumbent seeking reelection, we see that 42 percent voted for the challenger and 48 percent voted for the incumbent. In close elections, we again find that one side tends to benefit disproportionately, but there is no consistent party advantage to this pattern. As with the broader analysis of undecided voters, it is the out-party that tends to benefit. In landslide elections, partisans do come home, but the game is already over. The ANES data also offer little support for the notion that late deciders are traditionally Democrats.

What, then, is wrong with the common belief that undecided voters break for the challenger? Part of the answer is methodological: most analyses compare poll results to the vote. The result is partly a function of how undecided voters break, but it is also a function of polling error and shifts in the preferences of committed voters. Figure 4-2 adopts this more traditional (and, in my view, flawed) approach to analyzing undecided voters, comparing Gallup Poll surveys from the day before the election and from the week before the election with the final vote. The data indicate a slight tendency for the incumbent vote share to slip on Election Day. A slightly more significant tendency is for the challenger to gain support in the last week before the election. But

Figure 4-2. Movement in President's Vote Share in the Gallup Poll
as Election Day Approaches[a]

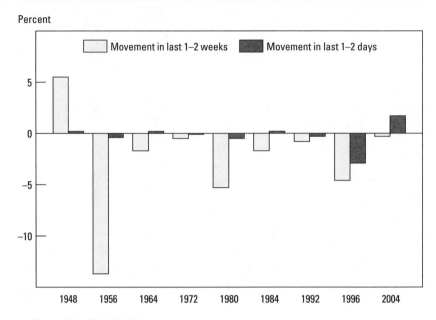

Percent

Source: Gallup Poll, 1948–2004.

a. Estimates are based on a comparison of the Republican share of the two-party vote over the specified time frame versus the final vote.

again, these data do not establish that undecided voters break one way or the other.

Part of the answer is also undoubtedly substantive: people who say they are undecided have not necessarily decided against the incumbent president. Given the amount of information available in presidential campaigns, it is certainly plausible that a voter might have serious misgivings about a president but still prefer him to the challenger.

But perhaps the most important part of the answer is that undecided voters are not where our attention should be focused. As seen in table 4-1, many undecideds are really nonvoters. Furthermore, some of the undecideds who do vote are actually reliable partisans who are simply late in coming home. I would argue that undecideds are loosely synonymous with swing voters only when all registrants vote and preferences adhere to the normal party vote. That is, when all partisans pledge to show up at the polls and declare their support for their party's nominees, we can be certain that undecided voters do not include wayward partisans who will be mobilized on or before Election Day. In all other instances, undecided voters include abstainers as well as a mixed assortment of partisans, some of whom have a genuine chance of defecting whereas others do not.

A Second Look at Political Science and Swing Voting

So if undecided voters are not necessarily swing voters, what can one recommend as a superior measure of swing voting? Looking again to the past, two research strands strike me as being particularly instructive: one strand focuses on "party switchers" and the other focuses on "floating voters." Let us begin with "party switchers." The notion that the electorate is composed of "standpatters," "new voters," and "party switchers" is a central point of V. O. Key's *The Responsible Electorate*.[13] This idea has its roots in some of the original survey research work of the Michigan school, and conceives of variance in elections as a product of the preferences of new voters and the relative proportion of partisans that defect from their party's nominee in a particular race.[14] Key estimates that party switchers constituted between 11 and 22 percent of the American electorate in the 1950s.[15] In addition, he argues that these voters are making a rational choice based on perceived differences between themselves and their party. This point is picked up by Richard Boyd, who examines the Reagan elections and finds that 15 percent of the electorate "switched" votes between 1980 and 1984, mostly as a result of evaluations of the candidates and appraisals of the economy.[16]

To the extent that party switchers from one election are more likely to defect in another, they strike me as synonymous with swing voters. But two subtle differences between these concepts stand out. First, most consultants (and probably more than a few political scientists) would classify those who seriously consider voting against their party's candidate as a swing voter. The fact that they ultimately vote in accord with their party identification does not mean they are like every other partisan. Second, a voter who supports the party's candidate in the current election but has defected in the past is not the same as a reliable partisan voter. More generally, I believe that measuring swing voting ought to include the previous behavior of individuals and groups to inform our understanding of their potential for "unusual" behavior in an unfolding election. I

13. Key (1966).
14. See Campbell, Gurin, and Miller (1954, pp. 11–27).
15. Key (1966, p. 19).
16. Boyd (1985).

want to identify those who might make a given election surprising. Otherwise swing voting becomes a post-hoc and descriptive concept.

In contrast, "floating voters" are defined as voters who are most susceptible to shifting back and forth between the parties during campaigns. Philip Converse's treatment of this concept is considered seminal, although the term predates him.[17] Particularly influential is his contention that voters whose preferences vary over the course of an election campaign are likely to be both relatively less attentive and less partisan. Cliff Zukin pursues this notion by trying to develop a more accurate measure of media exposure to test Converse's ideas about floating voters, but his examination of ANES data from 1952 to 1972 shows that media exposure is too widespread to account for the variance in vote choice stability.[18] He concludes that there is insufficient evidence to sustain the "information flow" argument. Johannes Pedersen examines the same data, however, and finds that less-informed voters are indeed more responsive to short-term stimuli, though not in every election.[19] More recently, John Zaller revisited the floating voters, arguing that they are distinguished, even defined, by their relatively low levels of political information.[20] As such, he finds that they disproportionately reward presidential successes in foreign policy and aggregate national economics (and, conversely, punish failures) and that they are acutely responsive to the ideological positions of the candidates.

As we consider swing voting, the main limitation of the "floating voter" literature is that it focuses exclusively on voters who appear to change their candidate preferences within a given campaign cycle. The problem is that the extent of preference consistency may simply be an artifact of when surveyors happen to interview a respondent, or may mask real ambivalence about an apparently consistent preference.[21]

More broadly, the question of whether swing voters look like party switchers, floating voters, or neither strikes me as an empirical matter. In this vein, it is important to note the differences between "floating voters" and "party switchers." On the one hand, "floaters" change their preferences during the campaign and are affected by short-term forces and elite cues conveyed by the news media. Although they move in response to the candidates' espoused ide-

17. Converse (1962); Daudt (1961); Zaller (2003).
18. Zukin (1977).
19. Pedersen (1978). See also Dobson and St. Angelo (1975) for a summary of floating voters in the ANES.
20. Zaller (2003).
21. Hillygus and Jackman (2003).

ologies, they are not ideologues; indeed, they are neither especially interested nor involved in the politics of the day. On the other hand, "switchers" cast votes out of line with their party identification and tend to do so because they either prefer another candidate's credentials or positions or are responding to some highly salient issue. These voters defect on the basis of their rather detailed and exceptional understanding of current political information.

A New Definition of Swing Voting

As we seek an improved definition of swing voting—one that allows us to consider the incidence of swing voting and whether certain groups are "swing" groups—let us begin by simplifying. One of the main sources of confusion with respect to swing voting is specifying the individual-level manifestation of what is viewed by campaign practitioners as a district- or county-level phenomenon. In other words, I have an individual-level conception of swing voting, whereas consultants consider it an aggregate-level phenomenon. This is not to suggest that swing voting is not driven by individuals' voting for different parties' candidates over some number of elections, since it clearly is. But for campaign professionals, such variance is only interesting if it affects the aggregate distribution of preferences; movement that cancels itself out is considered trivial. Because of this, and because it is difficult to accurately estimate an individual's voting record over a series of elections, professional swing voting analyses have tended to focus on aggregate-level results from states, counties, or precincts.[22]

I, therefore, begin with the theoretical assumption that every individual has a probability of voting for a particular party in a generic election. I further assume that swing voters are those whose probability of voting for one of the two major-party candidates in such an election is, ceteris paribus, close to 0.5. The first task, then, is to estimate the probability of a given individual's voting Democratic by examining her actual behavior over some subset of elections.

Ideally, one would want individual-level voting data for the same office over time, accompanied by detailed attitudinal and demographic information (more on this shortly). Traditional stand-alone surveys are of limited use, as they measure attitudes and behavior at a single point in time and, at best, might ask respondents how they voted in the last election. The panel surveys of the National Election Studies, however, offer a promising alternative. Following

22. Shea and Burton (2003).

their 2000 pre- and postelection survey, the ANES re-interviewed respondents in conjunction with the 2002 midterm and 2004 presidential elections. The 2000-to-2004 panel study provides us with reports of individual voting behavior for three presidential elections; contemporaneous reports about the 2000 and 2004 elections as well as each respondent's 2000 recollection of how he or she voted in 1996. Such information is available for 840 respondents, along with a wide array of theoretically intriguing explanatory variables.

In addition to the 2000-to-2004 panel study, the ANES conducted a similar panel for 1972 to 1976, which provides us with estimates of individual presidential voting behavior for 1968, 1972, and 1976. These two panel studies provide us an excellent opportunity to compare both the magnitude and correlates of swing voting over the span of the post–New Deal party system. The 1972 to 1976 study also allows me to ascertain the extent to which the groups that reputedly drove the restructuring of the New Deal coalition over social issues in the 1960s and 1970s actually did so, and continue to vacillate with respect to presidential voting preferences.

Because I wish to hold the type of election constant here, I focus on presidential elections. As suggested, the time frame is determined by the availability of panel surveys, but the panels used here encompass six elections with maximal variance in the outcome—one decisive Republican victory (1972), one decisive Democratic victory (1996), and four close races (1968, 1976, 2000, and 2004).

I use the summation of an individual respondent's votes across the three elections of each panel to ascertain that person's underlying probability of a partisan vote and to identify swing voters. This process is straightforward: anyone casting three consecutive votes for the same party is identified as a party voter, anyone abstaining in all three elections is a nonvoter, and everyone else is a swing voter.[23] Thus, voters who abstain or vote third party in one or two elections are swing voters, as are those who oscillate between the major-party candidates across elections. This variable serves as the critical descriptive and dependent variable in subsequent analyses.

How to Explain Swing Voting

In addition to clarifying and measuring swing voting, I am also interested in a more theoretical and coherent rendering of the variables that might plausi-

23. I rely on self-reported turnout because the ANES has not validated their turnout measure since 1988. The preponderance of evidence on the effect of using self-reported behavior suggests it slightly exaggerates the power of predictable voting correlates, such as education and income (see, for example, Presser 1990).

bly be expected to influence it. I proceed by grouping a wide range of poten-tial correlates into three separate categories, each rooted in a separate strand of the voting literature. Two of the three categories emphasize political and demographic characteristics. The other emphasizes the psychological vari-ables *interest* and *engagement*. The first category encompasses groups whose departure from the Democratic Party's New Deal coalition has been offered as an explanation for the heightened competitiveness of the post–New Deal system. In other words, they measure the degree to which swing voters are members of groups whose long-standing partisan predispositions have shifted over the past forty years, largely over social issues.[24] This category includes Catholics, members of union households, white southerners, west-erners, seniors, college graduates, members of higher-income households, and (to a much lesser extent) Latinos and Jews. I also include African Amer-icans, who have presumably moved even more strongly toward the Demo-crats, and men, whose vote appears to have become more variable.[25]

In the second category I include groups who are "cross-pressured" by the contrary ideological pulls of different components of their identities. The critical idea behind this category, derived from the Columbia studies, is that some voters are more likely to favor, say, one party on economic issues but the other party on social issues. Many of the groups tagged by the media and political pundits as swing groups fit nicely under this heading. Hence, into this category I place those in the middle third of the income distribution, those with some college education, suburbanites, and rural dwellers, along with "soccer moms," "waitress moms," and "office park dads."[26]

The third category uses psychological variables, political interest and knowledge, to explain swing voting. This draws on Converse's notion that voters who are engaged enough to be exposed to the political debate but are the least resistant to political messages are the most likely to be persuaded. For presidential elections, exposure ought to reach the lowest rungs of the information ladder, so the expectation is that the least informed are the most likely to be swing voters.[27] Although I am most interested in individual-level psychological predispositions, I do test for the possibility that certain groups are disproportionately likely to have these predispositions. Thus, I examine

24. See Petrocik (1981).
25. See Kaufmann and Petrocik (1999).
26. These categories are obviously not mutually exclusive.
27. This obviously differs from Zaller's prediction that voters in the middle of the infor-mation scale are most likely to be persuaded. As stated earlier, though, Zaller focuses on U.S. Senate elections, where exposure is less extensive (see Zaller 2003).

political independents, the young (under thirty years of age), the less educated and affluent, and those who otherwise express lower levels of political
interest and engagement. My expectation is that swing voting will be most
affected by psychological attributes, whereas membership in specific groups
will be significantly less influential. This expectation is stronger for the 2000-
to-2004 panel than for the 1968-to-1976 panel because contemporary party
coalitions are more diverse than those of the 1960s.

Of course, it is possible that sociological and psychological factors work
together. For example, it might be that more informed and interested soccer
moms are relatively likely to be swing voters. Thus, I allow political information to interact with group membership so that I can estimate the influence
of engagement on swing voting within and across groups. Given my preference for psychological explanations of swing voting, I am skeptical of interactive effects. If they exist, however, I would expect that informed members
of groups with strong historical attachments to a particular party should realize even deeper commitment to the group preference (for example, informed
African Americans for Democrats). For groups without strong historical
party attachments, or who have been targeted by both major parties, I expect
that heightened information could lead to candidate and issue-specific preferences (for example, informed younger voters are swing voters).

What about Issues?

It is reasonable, of course, to question the absence of issue positions in the
models of swing voting. In my view, issue and candidate dynamics drive the
direction of swing voting in a specific election, but have only an indirect effect
on who is a swing voter. For example, swing voters voted for Ronald Reagan
in 1984 but turned around and voted for Bill Clinton in 1996; although their
candidate preferences were blown in certain directions by the prevailing
political winds, swing voters were the same people in these disparate elections. Put another way, political context tells us how swing voters behave in a
given election, but sheds little light on the underlying nature of swing voters.[28] I assume broader dynamics are dominant here—particularly those

---

28. It is possible that the specific appeals of a candidate can induce someone whose underlying party vote probability is 0.90 to vote the other way. I believe this to be quite rare, however. In addition, as a practical matter, such a behavior would shift our estimate of the
underlying vote probability closer to 0.50 (as our swing voter definition is empirically derived)
and could result in a reclassification of this voter's status as a swing voter.

involving party system reactions to new issues and cross pressures that are at the core of these analyses.

Swing voters thus form a distinct group, whose membership is roughly consistent from election to election. I believe the underlying probability of voting Democratic (or, conversely, Republican) is conditioned by the parties' positions on the dominant issues of the era. For example, someone who is liberal on social welfare issues but conservative on social issues—the dominant issues of the post–New Deal party system—is likely to have a Democratic vote probability of about 0.50 (assuming she cares equally about both issue dimensions). I have similar expectations for someone whose social identity draws on politically opposite groups. In this way, issues are fundamental to my understanding of swing voters. But psychological predispositions and sociopolitical identities are prior to issue positions; as such, they are my main independent variables.

How Many Swing Voters Are There?

Recall the conventional wisdom advanced throughout the 2004 presidential election campaign: that the nation was bitterly divided into two polarized camps. The election, we were told, was all about mobilization, while swing voters were an endangered species. The data, however, suggest that 2004 is the endpoint to an era in which one-quarter of the electorate could reasonably be called "swing."

More precisely, table 4-3 shows that 24 percent of Americans qualify as swing voters on the basis of their behavior in the presidential elections of 1996, 2000, and 2004. In fact, the electorate seems loosely divided into quartiles, with one fourth voting straight Republican (26 percent), one fourth voting straight Democratic (27 percent), one fourth not voting (23 percent), and one fourth swinging. A more detailed examination demonstrates that 54 percent of Americans voted a straight party line over these three elections, and another 20 percent voted mostly along party lines (11 percent voted for two of three Republicans, 8 percent voted for two of three Democrats).[29] Only a tiny fraction of the electorate voted mostly independent (2 percent) or Republican, Democratic, and independent (3 percent).

The bottom line, however, is that swing voting is hardly the scarce commodity it is sometimes made out to be. More important, given the incidence

29. "Two of three party votes" includes those who twice voted a party line but abstained in the other election.

Table 4-3. Swing Voting in Past Presidential Election Cycles
Percent

Three presidential votes	1968–76	1996–2004
Collapsed		
Voted straight Republican	30	26
Voted straight Democratic	15	27
Didn't vote	12	23
Swing	44	24
Detailed breakdown of swing voters		
Voted straight Republican	30	26
Voted mostly Republican	21	11
Voted straight Democratic	15	27
Voted mostly Democratic	13	8
Voted mostly Independent	1	1
Mostly didn't vote	12	23
Voted one Republican, one Democrat, one independent	9	3
N	902	826

Source: Based on national panel surveys conducted by the American National Election Studies, Center for Political Studies, University of Michigan, 2000–04 and 1972–76.

of swing voting in the electorate and the even distribution of party-line voters (26 percent Republican to 27 percent Democratic), swing voters were critical to deciding presidential elections. Clinton in 1996 and Bush in 2000 and 2004 *had* to carry swing voters to win.

The impact of swing voters in the elections of 1968, 1972, and 1976 is more complicated. Given the political turbulence of the late sixties and early seventies, it is unsurprising that the level of swing voting in the elections of 1968, 1972, and 1976 would be relatively high.[30] Still, table 4-3's 44 percent swing voting estimate represents an enormous proportion of the electorate. The distribution of voters is even more surprising—30 percent voted straight Republican across these elections, whereas only 15 percent voted straight Democratic. A full 9 percent voted for independent, Republican, and Democratic candidates over these three elections (presumably, the lion's share of these supported Wallace, then Nixon, and then Carter). Thus, although there were more swing voters in these elections, the distribution of party-line voters was less balanced—one could win without carrying swing voters in the late 1960s and early 1970s. More generally, this was a remarkable transition period in American politics: at the tail end of the New Deal party system—a

30. See, for example, Bartels (2000).

Figure 4-3. Deviation of Major Voter Groups from Swing Voting Average, 2000–04

Percent

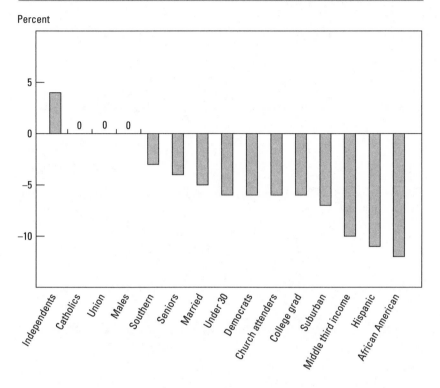

Source: American National Election Studies, 2000–04 panel.

system characterized by Democratic dominance—Republicans had crafted an advantage in presidential elections. Note also the relatively low proportion of nonvoters: 12 percent, compared to 23 percent in the 1996-to-2004 data.

Who Is a Swing Voter?

Despite the popular fascination with angry white males and soccer moms, I expect that contemporary swing voters are voters who are relatively less interested, less engaged, and less informed about politics than the average voter. Figure 4-3 confirms this expectation, showing that among all our groups only political independents are obviously more likely to be swing voters in the 1996, 2000, and 2004 elections. In contrast, the list of groups that are less likely to swing

Figure 4-4. Deviation of Major Voting Groups from Swing Voting Average, 1972–76

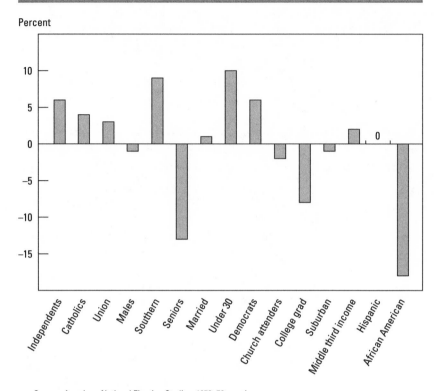

Source: American National Election Studies, 1972–76 panel.

across these elections is extensive: African Americans (15 percent less likely to be swing voters than the average voter), Hispanics (11 percent less likely), those from middle-income households (10 percent less likely), suburbanites (7 percent less likely), college graduates (6 percent less likely), church attenders (6 percent less likely), Democrats (6 percent less likely), those under thirty years of age (6 percent less likely), married people (6 percent less likely), seniors (4 percent less likely), and southerners (3 percent less likely).

Recall that I also expect social-group identities to be more relevant for swing voting in the 1968-to-1976 elections than in the 2000-to-2004 elections. Figure 4-4 bears this out as well, clearly demonstrating that independents were not the only wellspring of swing voters in these elections. Those under thirty years of age (10 percent more likely to be swing voters), southerners (9 percent), Democrats (6 percent), Catholics (4 percent), and members of union households (3 percent) are all well above the average level of swing voting across these races. Furthermore, these tendencies are consistent with the common perception that the white South was particularly volatile during this period of time, as race and civil rights issues cross-cut established ties with the Democratic Party in 1968 and 1972, only to be temporarily reaffirmed with the candidacy of native son (and born-again Christian) Jimmy Carter in 1976.

Do these core findings hold up to more rigorous multivariate testing? For both 1996 to 2004 and 1968 to 1976, I use a binary logistic regression estimator to model direct and interactive effects (see the table in the appendix for complete results). I include all two-way interactions between information level and other explanatory variables, which allows me to gauge the conditional influence of political engagement and other sociopolitical variables on swing voting.[31] For 1996 to 2004, the model indicates that political independence and political information are critical in predicting swing voting. Figure 4-5 shows the significant effects from the 1996-to-2004 elections. When interactive information effects are taken into consideration, political independence actually increases in significance while the direct influence of information decreases slightly. At the same time, I find that both waitress moms and wealthy, informed voters are slightly more likely to be swing voters.

Interestingly, wealthy, less-informed voters are less likely to be swing voters. Recall that I expected to see informed members of core party groups emerge as *less* likely to be swing voters—this is only partially borne out by the data. Informed African Americans, informed Jews, informed white southerners, informed union members, and informed seniors, for instance, are all

---

31. Interaction effects are modeled as multiplicative, with the information measure consisting of a five-point scale and all other explanatory variables being coded dichotomously. There are two possible objections to this. First, some have recently argued that the selective use of interactive terms in models can result in biased estimates (see especially Braumoeller 2004). Although I take this point, I do not believe it appropriate to include all possible interactive terms in the model. A selection of fuller two-way and three-way interaction effect models suggests that the estimated effect differences with the two-way models presented in the appendix are minimal. Second, there is a long-standing statistical and econometric debate about the interpretation of interactions due to the nonlinearity of logit estimation procedures. Initially I dealt with this issue by recoding the political information variable dichotomously (high information versus all else) and rerunning the models. The magnitude of some estimates changes, but not significantly. I then estimated models for different categories of informed voters and compared the "marginal effects" across categories. This did alter some of the substantive findings. Most notably, party identification and social status variables gained explanatory power.

Figure 4-5. Probit Estimates of the Effect of Voter Characteristics on Probability of Being a Swing Voter, 1996–2004

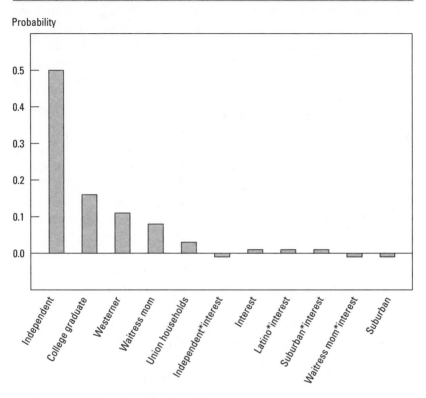

Source: American National Election Studies, 2000–04 panel.

more likely to swing. Conversely, informed Catholics are less likely, as are informed males.

Recall also that I had expected to see informed members of targeted groups emerge as the most likely to be swing voters—this is often (but not always) the case. For example, informed suburbanites, informed members of middle-income households, informed younger voters, and informed college graduates are all more likely to be swing voters, whereas informed Latinos, informed waitress moms, informed office park dads, and informed soccer moms are less likely. Moreover, these mixed results are all based on regression coefficients that fall slightly below standard levels of statistical significance, and thus must be interpreted with caution.

For the elections from 1968 to 1976, information and political independence dominate the model, with the former driving nonswing behavior and the latter driving swing voting. The effect of political independence disappears, however, when one allows information to condition the influence of sociopolitical and other engagement factors. In other words, informed members of several sociopolitical groups are relatively likely to identify as political independents, and it is these people who drive swing voting across this series of elections. Almost all of the statistically significant effects disappear as well, although several marginally significant effects remain (informed people, informed African Americans, white southerners, those in the top-income third, informed college graduates, and office park dads are less likely to swing, whereas informed people under thirty years of age, informed westerners, and informed office park dads are more likely to swing).

Conclusion

Taking into account all of the data, three important points emerge. First, conventional news media accounts of swing voting—most of which focus on undecided voters—do little to help us understand presidential election dynamics. This is partly because following undecided voter percentages gives undue influence to sampling error and partisan mobilization while ignoring the preferences of true swing voters. Undecideds are not necessarily swing voters; some are partisans, some are nonvoters, and others are truly persuadable.

A second point is that although the level of swing voting declined between the 1968-to-1976 period and the 1996-to-2004 period, 25 percent of Americans remain swing voters. Furthermore, the even distribution of Republican and Democratic party-line voters ensures that swing voters decide American national elections. But this fact has produced an ironic reaction. Political consultants readily acknowledge the practical importance of swing voters in contemporary election campaigns, but many also believe that these voters are difficult to reach and even tougher to win over.[32] They argue that swing voters tend to be located in the middle of the political-ideological spectrum, meaning that persuading them to support a specific candidate is best accomplished by championing moderate, mainstream issues and policy positions. It is difficult, however, to grab headlines or fire passions with moderate, mainstream issues. In addition, by laboring to tempt swing voters to the polls, a candidate runs the risk of alienating his

32. Shea and Burton (2003).

base. This perspective has led some consultants to question the wisdom of chasing this elusive quarry.[33]

Third and finally, understanding the propensity of individual Americans to be swing voters across some subset of presidential elections depends heavily on the psychological variables of political independence and voter engagement and (to a slightly lesser degree) on the interaction between political-demographic and engagement variables. Group identities, important for swing voting in the 1968-to-1976 elections, are much less so in the 1996-to-2004 elections. I think it is especially important to observe that the groups labeled swing voters by consultants and the news media over the last few cycles only occasionally measure up as such. Soccer moms, Latinos, and rural voters are simply not swing voters.

I do not wish to overstate things. The 1996-to-2004 data indicate that, all other things being equal, independents, men, Catholics, waitress moms, and office park dads have marginally higher probabilities of being swing voters. In short, these findings *suggest* there is a political demography to swing voting, but they also tell us that these tendencies are conditioned by political independence and political engagement.

All of this again raises the question of whether swing voters are worth the trouble. The robust relationships between swing voting and political independence (positive) and political engagement (negative) suggest that campaigns may actually be well advised to scale back their efforts to reach out to swing voters. Campaigns have limited resources, and the commitment necessary to reach independent, inattentive swing voters may be prohibitive. Moreover, such outreach might well be swamped by larger events or circumstances (the prevailing wind that tends to dominate swing voter impressions). This logic has not been lost on recent presidential campaigns: the 2000 Bush campaign spent 75 percent of its advertising and contacting budget on "persuadable" voters; in 2004, it spent 50 percent.[34]

Setting these practical matters aside for the moment, I would feel remiss were I not to return to the broader theoretical question of whether swing voters more closely resemble Key's informed, engaged "party switchers" or Converse's uninformed, unengaged "floating voters." Here the data clearly support Converse. The significance of political independence as an explanation

33. See Adam Nagourney, "Political Parties Shift Emphasis to Core Voters," *New York Times*, September 11, 2003.

34. Thomas Edsall and Mark Grimaldi, "GOP Made Better Use of Its Millions," *Washington Post*, December 28, 2004, p. A1.

for swing voting in both models suggests that swing voters are relatively unlikely to correspond to Key's sophisticated, issue-driven "party switchers." This tentative conclusion suggests an obvious but important limitation of the present analysis: political context matters. Swing voting is determined by the receptiveness of the voter to contextual information, which is determined not only by political-demographic and engagement characteristics but also by the interaction of these characteristics with the nature of the information that arises in a particular race. Put another way, a voter who happens to be Latina was more likely to be persuadable in 2000 if she was exposed to issues and information that Latina voters are relatively more likely to care about. By the same token, a swing voter who happens to be Catholic was less likely to be persuadable in 2000 if she was exposed to issues and information that Catholics are relatively less likely to care about. Someone with an otherwise low probability of swing voting might become a swing voter if the issue context hits home.

Table 4-A. Logistic Regression Models of Swing Voting[a]

	1968–76		1996–2004	
	Full model	*Non-interactive model*	*Full model*	*Non-interactive model*
New Deal groups				
Male	−0.208	−0.048	0.612	0.399*
Male*informed	0.264	. . .	−0.387	. . .
African American	−0.449	−1.189***	−3.080	−0.739
African American*informed	−1.625	. . .	3.422	. . .
Latino	. . .	. . .	0.966	−0.300
Latino*informed	. . .	. . .	−2.330	. . .
Catholic	−0.430	0.087	0.816	0.030
Catholic*informed	0.897	. . .	−1.171	. . .
Jewish	0.028	0.325	−1.224	−0.306
Jewish*informed	0.337	. . .	1.107	. . .
White southerner	−1.054	−0.529*	−0.428	−0.112
White southerner*informed	0.846	. . .	1.040	. . .
Westerner	−0.769	−0.050	0.098	0.288
Westerner*informed	1.166	. . .	0.225	. . .
Union	0.800	−0.079	−0.338	−0.022
Union*informed	−1.472	. . .	0.554	. . .
Senior	−0.870	−1.109***	−0.694	−0.470*
Senior*informed	−0.512	. . .	0.263	. . .
Top income third	−1.323*	−0.837**	−1.628*	−0.230
Top income third*informed	0.871	. . .	1.942*	. . .
College grad	1.411	−0.608**	−0.667	−0.351
College grad*informed	−2.878**	. . .	0.390	. . .

(continued)

Table 4-A. Logistic Regression Models of Swing Voting[a] *(continued)*

	1968–76		1996–2004	
	Full model	*Non-interactive model*	*Full model*	*Non-interactive model*
Cross-pressured groups				
Suburban	−0.770	−0.201	0.347	−0.071
Suburban*informed	0.868	...	0.388	...
Rural	0.359	0.166	1.206	−0.505
Rural*informed	−0.337	...	−2.365	...
Middle income third	−0.973	−0.804**	−1.001	−0.310
Middle income third*informed	0.442	...	0.990	...
Some college	−0.048	−0.317	−0.509	−0.177
Some college*informed	−0.584	...	0.565	...
Soccer mom	0.254	0.617	0.158	−0.476
Soccer mom*informed	0.651	...	−0.792	...
Waitress mom	−0.513	−0.486	3.508*	0.037
Waitress mom*informed	0.040	...	−6.000	...
Office park dad	−0.835	0.145	1.307	0.264
Office park dad*informed	1.664	...	−1.454	...
Engagement groups				
Informed	−1.291	−0.729*	−1.476	−1.488***
Independent	−0.063	0.413**	1.729*	1.112**
Independent*informed	0.795	...	−0.950	...
Under thirty	−0.560	0.316	0.578	0.367
Under thirty*informed	1.369	...	1.727	...
Total cases	791	791	646	646
−2 log likelihood	995.84	1,017.59	721.11	739.15
Chi-square	100.56***	78.82***	70.37***	52.33***
Nagelkerke R^2	0.16	0.13	0.15	0.11

Source: ANES Panel Studies, 1972–76 and 2000–04.

a. Nonvoters are excluded from the analyses. Entries represent parameter estimates derived from binary logistic regression analyses.

*Significant at 0.05; **significant at 0.01 level; ***significant at 0.001. All tests are two-tailed.

References

Bartels, Larry M. 2000. "Partisanship and Voting Behavior, 1952–1996." *American Journal of Political Science* 44, no. 1: 35–50.

Berelson, Bernard R., Paul F. Lazarsfeld, and William N. McPhee. 1954. *Voting: A Study of Opinion Formation in a Presidential Campaign.* University of Chicago Press.

Boyd, Richard W. 1985. "Electoral Change in the United States and Great Britain." *British Journal of Political Science* 15, no. 4: 517–28.

Braumoeller, Bear. 2004. "Hypothesis Testing and Multiplicative Interaction Terms." *International Organization* 58 (Fall): 807–20.

Campbell, Angus, Peter E. Converse, William E. Miller, and Donald E. Stokes. 1960. *The American Voter*. New York: Wiley.

Campbell, Angus, Gerald Gurin, and Warren Miller. 1954. *The Voter Decides*. Evanston, Ill.: Peterson.

Converse, Philip. 1962. "Information Flow and the Stability of Partisan Attitudes." *Public Opinion Quarterly* 26, no. 4: 578–99.

Daudt, Hans. 1961. *Floating Voters and the Floating Vote: A Critical Analysis of American and English Election Studies*. Leiden, Netherlands: H. E. Stenfert Kroese.

Dobson, Douglas, and Douglas St. Angelo. 1975. "Party Identification and the Floating Vote: Some Dynamics." *American Political Science Review* 69, no. 2: 481–90.

Downs, Anthony. 1957. *An Economic Theory of Democracy*. New York: Harper and Row.

Hillygus, D. Sunshine, and Simon Jackman. 2003. "Voter Decision Making in Election 2000." *American Journal of Political Science* 47, no. 4: 583–96.

Kaufmann, Karen M., and John R. Petrocik. 1999. "The Changing Politics of American Men: Understanding the Sources of the Gender Gap." *American Journal of Political Science* 43, no. 3: 164–87.

Key, V. O., Jr. 1966. *The Responsible Electorate: Rationality in Presidential Voting 1936–1960*. Harvard University Press.

Lazarsfeld, P. F., B. Berelson, and H. Gaudet. 1948. *The People's Choice: How the Voter Makes Up His Mind in a Presidential Campaign*. 2nd ed. Columbia University Press.

Panagakis, Nick. 1989. "Incumbent Races: Closer Than They Appear." *Polling Report*, February 27.

Pedersen, Johannes T. 1978. "Political Involvement and Partisan Change in Presidential Elections." *American Journal of Political Science* 22, no. 1: 18–30.

Petrocik, John R. 1981. *Party Coalitions*. University of Chicago Press.

Presser, Stanley. 1990. "Can Changes in Context Reduce Voter Overreporting in Surveys?" *Public Opinion Quarterly* 54, no. 4: 586–93.

Shea, Daniel M., and Michael John Burton. 2003. *Campaign Craft: The Strategies, Tactics, and Art of Political Campaign Management*. New York: Praeger.

Wlezien, Christopher, and Robert S. Erikson. 2002. "The Timeline of Presidential Election Campaigns." *Journal of Politics* 64, no. 4: 969–93.

Zaller, John. 2003. "Floating Voters in U.S. Presidential Elections, 1948–2000." In *Studies in Public Opinion: Gauging Attitudes, Nonattitudes, Measurement Error, and Change*, edited by William E. Saris and Paul M. Sniderman, pp. 166–212. Princeton University Press.

Zukin, Cliff. 1977. "A Reconsideration of the Effects of Information on Partisan Stability." *Public Opinion Quarterly* 41, no. 2: 244–54.

five
Swing Voters in Subnational Campaigns

Jeffrey M. Stonecash

This chapter takes up a question raised by William Mayer in chapter 1: Does the concept of a swing voter apply to nonpresidential elections? As the reader may already have noticed, all of the data and analyses in chapters 1, 2, 3, and 4 are based on presidential elections; the same is true of chapters 6 and 7. In focusing on presidential elections, these authors are faithfully reflecting popular usage of the term *swing voter*. For example, all of the media stories about swing voters that Mayer cites in his chapter are stories about the presidential campaign.[1]

Yet as interesting and consequential as presidential elections are, they are only a small part of the U.S. electoral universe. Every two years, Americans elect 435 members of the House of Representatives and one-third of the Senate, along with a slew of state, local, and county officials. Is it meaningful to talk about swing voters in elections on the state or congressional levels?

In one sense, the answer is surely yes. If a swing voter is defined as someone who is potentially persuadable, whose vote choice might be influenced by

---

1. In light of the general theme developed in this chapter, it is worth noting that most of the stories about swing voters that were not about the presidential election dealt with unusually high-profile Senate races, such as the 2000 contest between Hillary Clinton and Rick Lazio in New York. See, for example, William Goldschlag, "Clinton and Lazio Lock Horns Tonight," *New York Daily News,* September 13, 2000, p. 22; Andrew Miga, "Hillary Failing to Shake Lazio in Senate Race," *Boston Herald,* September 17, 2000, p. 4; Randal C. Archibold, "Mrs. Clinton's Primary Opponent Backs Lazio," *New York Times,* October 6, 2000, p. B10.

the campaign, then there is no doubt that such people exist in virtually every conceivable type of election. Indeed, as I will show later in this chapter, the percentage of potentially persuadable voters may well be higher in the typical congressional election than in the average presidential campaign. The more relevant—and more difficult—question is: Can we define and delimit the set of voters whose preferences might be changed?

The techniques used to identify swing voters in the preceding chapters all assume that voters have at least a minimum level of familiarity with both of the major candidates. This is most obviously the case with Mayer's thermometer-ratings measure, which, as he notes, can only be computed for respondents who are able to provide ratings for both the Republican and Democratic presidential candidates. Less obviously, the same is true of the approach taken by the Gallup, Pew, and Annenberg surveys, which ask voters who express a preference for one candidate whether there is any chance that they will change their minds. Although most voters in a congressional or state representative election would probably be willing to answer this type of question, it is not clear how meaningful the answer would be if a voter lacked significant information about one or both candidates. Except for the most hard-core partisans, voters who know nothing about a candidate have no basis for saying that they would never vote for that candidate. Perhaps if they did learn something, they would find the candidate to be a quite attractive alternative.

Identifying Swing Voters in Low Information Elections

Presidential and nonpresidential elections differ in a number of ways, but one of the most important and reliable differences concerns the amount of information that voters have about the major candidates. In presidential campaigns, most voters begin the fall campaign with a fairly high level of information and reasonably developed images of the major-party candidates. Given this starting point, campaign strategists often use polls to determine what types of voters are ambivalent and what issues and candidate qualities matter most to them. These results are then used to guide the substance of the campaign's ads, speeches, and other forms of communication; subsequent polls determine whether images and support by issue positions shift as expected in response to the campaign themes pursued. For example, in the 2004 presidential campaign, the Swift Boat group sought to create doubts about John Kerry's Vietnam War hero credentials in order to diminish public evaluations of his character and reduce his support within selected electoral groups such as veterans.

While this framework for assessing the role of swing voters is appropriate for national contests, in most subnational campaigns the assumption of high levels of information about candidates does not hold. Many subnational races begin with candidates, even incumbents, who are not well known. The first and often only challenge for such candidates is to boost their name recognition higher than that of their opponent. When voters are faced with a choice between one candidate they have heard of and one they have not heard of, unless the information is disproportionately negative most voters will go with the one they have heard about. Many campaigns might begin with the presumption that those registered or enrolled in a party will eventually vote for the candidate of that party, but this is not necessarily a safe assumption. Voters who have no awareness or image of the candidates are often amenable to being moved to support either candidate.

Consider, for example, the data in table 5-1, drawn from a survey of a county legislative race in upstate New York that pitted a long-term incumbent against a challenger. Survey respondents were asked whether they had a favorable or unfavorable impression of each candidate, but were also explicitly given the option of saying that they had never heard of the candidate or didn't know enough about him or her to have an opinion (the exact wording of the question is presented in table 5-1). Those who had some impression of a candidate, favorable or unfavorable, are grouped together as knowing the candidate. Those who had no opinion or had never heard of a candidate are also grouped together. Then respondents are sorted by whether they knew both candidates, just one candidate, or neither. The overall distribution of these categories is shown to the right.

Two points are particularly worth noting. First, the extent of name recognition is not high, even though the poll was conducted among likely voters. The incumbent county legislator had been in office eighteen years, yet only 56 percent of likely voters knew him well enough to say that they had a favorable or unfavorable impression of him. Second, differentials in awareness had a huge impact on the vote. Respondents who knew both candidates (the top row) divided fairly evenly: 43 percent for the incumbent, 40 percent for the challenger. Those who didn't know either candidate (bottom row) were also reasonably even: 31 percent for the incumbent to 20 percent for the challenger. The crucial matter, however, is that 46 percent of the respondents knew the incumbent but not the challenger, whereas only 4 percent knew the challenger and not the incumbent. Voters who know one candidate and not the other (second and third rows) go overwhelmingly (more than 70 percent) for the one they know, so having greater name recognition is very valu-

Table 5-1. Vote Choice by Voters' Awareness of Candidates in a County Legislative Race
Percent

	Vote choice (percentaged across)			
	Incumbent	Challenger	Don't know	Percentage of sample
Know both candidates[a]	43	40	17	10
Know incumbent but not challenger	71	9	20	46
Know challenger but not incumbent	17	75	8	4
Don't know either candidate	31	20	49	40

Source: Poll of county legislative race conducted by the author.
a. The question asked was "Do you have a favorable or unfavorable impression of _____ or have you not heard of the person or have heard of them but have no opinion about them?" Those who had a favorable or unfavorable impression of a candidate were classified as "knowing" that candidate.

able. The goal in many subnational races is to create precisely this kind of mismatch in name recognition. And a swing voter, in turn, is anyone who can be provided with information about and made aware of one candidate while the other campaign fails to meet this threshold.

Thus, although swing, or persuadable, voters undoubtedly exist in subnational elections, it is considerably more difficult to say in advance or on the basis of just one poll who these voters are or how many of them there are. Identifying the most persuadable voters often requires a campaign strategist or survey analyst to take into account the particular circumstances of each election and sometimes to make plausible assumptions about how much new information the voters are likely to learn and how they are likely to react if they do learn it.

The rest of this chapter explores the nature and incidence of swing voters in different types of subnational campaigns. To illustrate the specific types of challenges and opportunities available in these campaigns, results from specific races will be cited. All poll results come from my own experiences polling for candidates in the upstate New York region. I have conducted polls for candidates for Congress, the state legislature, county executive, district attorney, mayor, judge, county legislator, and city council since 1987.

Subnational races vary enormously in the initial positions of the candidates and the political context, but there are some situations that occur fairly regularly. In each of these situations, the central variables are the visibility and depth of information voters have about the candidates. The following situations are common:

—A candidate is almost entirely unknown, either because he or she is new to electoral politics or because the candidate is an incumbent who has received very little press coverage. The latter description applies to many state, county, and city legislators.

—A candidate is an incumbent with a high level of name recognition, but polling indicates that a substantial percentage of the electorate say that they do not have much specific information about the incumbent's record.

—A candidate who is fairly well known faces a largely unknown challenger and must decide whether to ignore the opponent on the assumption that he or she will never become well known or assume that the opponent has the resources to become substantially better known and consequently take steps to define the opponent before he or she can define him- or herself.

—Both candidates have fairly high visibility but voters have little depth of information about a candidate's opponent, so the challenge is to try to alter the image of the opponent.

New Candidate with Low Visibility

It is fairly common that when a new candidate enters a race the individual is largely unknown to the vast majority of potential voters. The major challenge such a candidate faces is just getting voters to know that he or she exists. Figure 5-1 tracks the level of name recognition and favorability ratings of a first-time candidate for the New York state legislature between May and October 2002. This individual was seeking a seat that had been held by his father for two decades. Father and son had the same last name but different first names. The data in figure 5-1 are based on responses to the standard question, often asked at the beginning of a poll: "I'd like to read you the names of some people in public life. For each name, could you please tell me whether your impression of that person is favorable or unfavorable? If you have never heard of someone, or you don't know enough to have an opinion, just indicate that."

This question can be used to divide respondents into three major categories, according to how much they claim to know about a given candidate:

—*Never heard of the candidate.* At the lowest level of information, of course, are people who say they have simply never heard of the candidate.

—*No opinion.* One level up are those voters who have heard of the candidate but don't have enough information to evaluate him or her.

—*Able to rate the candidate.* The most knowledgeable voters are those who are actually able to provide a favorable or unfavorable evaluation of the candidate.

Figure 5-1. Favorable and Unfavorable Ratings of Republican State Assembly Candidate among Republicans

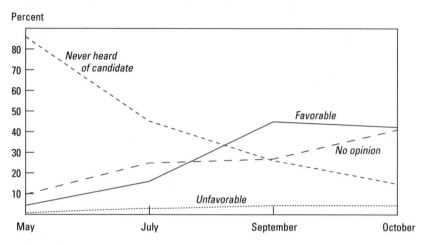

Percent

Source: Surveys conducted by the author.

The responses shown in figure 5-1 are those of Republicans only, for two reasons. First, the candidate was forced to run in a primary because another local Republican was also seeking the seat and was unwilling to step aside for the son of the sitting legislator. Second, tracking these responses within the candidate's own party is revealing of the visibility problems new candidates often face. This candidate had a father with long experience in party politics, yet even with that advantage, only 5 percent of likely Republican voters could provide any rating, favorable or unfavorable, of the candidate. Faced with this situation, the candidate made a commitment to conducting door-to-door visits with every likely Republican voter in the district. We acquired the Board of Elections file of registrants and selected all Republicans with a record of voting frequently, sorting them by address for each street, and the candidate then devoted every evening during the summer to door-to-door visits. Two direct-mail pieces were also sent to these voters. Newspaper coverage, by contrast, was very limited.

We took another poll among Republicans in July to track the candidate's progress in increasing his visibility. His progress was significant in one regard but painfully slow in another. The number who had never heard of him declined from 85 percent to 45 percent, but much of this decline only resulted in an increase in the percentage with no opinion. The percentage of respondents who were able to rate the candidate had increased to 19 percent, with almost all of these ratings favorable. The direct mail and door-to-door visits continued through the primary in mid-September, which the candidate won. By the third week in September, his "never-heard-of" percentage among Republicans was down to 26 percent and the "no opinion" percentage was at 27 percent. By late October, he had made further progress and the never-heard-of percentage was down to 14 percent with 40 percent having no opinion. The candidate's rise in visibility within his own party took extensive work, yet even then only half of likely voters had any impression of him.

The good news for the Republican candidate was the difficulty his Democratic opponent had in increasing his visibility. By late October, 32 percent of our survey respondents had a clear impression of the Democratic candidate, 41 percent had no opinion, and 26 percent had never heard of him. The Republican candidate eventually won the election.

This race illustrates the major challenge that new candidates face, even within their own party, in increasing their visibility during a campaign. This candidate worked very hard, yet even with all that work, only 38 percent of all likely voters were able to say that they had a favorable or unfavorable opinion of him. In the same October poll, 48 percent of Republicans said that they would vote for this candidate, but this result could not be taken for granted. At the beginning of this campaign, most voters were probably "up for grabs." That is, without a major effort by the candidate, he would not have been able to count on strong support from his own party. The candidate's campaign did send out some "contrast"-type direct-mail pieces that presented the Republican as against tax cuts and the Democrat as in favor of taxes, but in large part the direct mail consisted of oversized postcards that presented pictures, biographical information, and a few issue positions. The image of well-known candidates using subtle issue messages to move voters has little relevance to such contests.

Incumbent with High Name Recognition but Limited Specific Information

Incumbents are generally assumed to have high name recognition and consequently a considerable advantage. That may be true, but many incumbents still face a situation in which voters have little concrete sense of their record in office. To the extent that voters lack this kind of information about the incumbent, it is possible for a challenger to "fill out" the incumbent's image and thus *define* the incumbent in a way that is favorable to the challenger. For example, in a political climate like that of the 2006 elections, when George

Bush's approval rating was very low, a Republican incumbent could readily be portrayed as just a local version of Bush. For voters who lack information about the incumbent, such an appeal might be enough to swing them to the challenger.

To try to assess the extent to which this potential might exist in an incumbent, I often ask the job approval question in the following way: "Do you approve or disapprove of the job [elected official] is doing as [office], or don't you know enough to judge that?" For one incumbent congressman who had been in office for over a decade, 34 percent of likely voters chose the "don't know enough" response in April of 2006. Among those with an opinion, the ratio of approve to disapprove responses was very good; but with one-third of the voters admitting that they didn't really know much about the incumbent, there was considerable potential for a challenger to connect the incumbent to George Bush and thus attract votes. In this type of situation, the percentage of possible swing voters is fairly high.

Fairly Well-Known Candidate Facing Largely Unknown Challenger

Many incumbents face challengers who begin the campaign with very little name recognition. An important early decision for the incumbent's campaign is to assess the political climate and, in particular, the possibility that the challenger will be able to raise large amounts of money. If the political climate for the incumbent is not positive and it appears likely that the challenger will raise sufficient funds to create a serious race, then the incumbent may wish to use his or her resources to define the opponent early in the race, before the opponent can do this. If done effectively, this can prevent the challenger from becoming a viable alternative, even if he or she does succeed in increasing his or her visibility. If the challenger is not defined and the political climate is not favorable to the incumbent, the challenger may be able to pull a large number of what might initially appear to be safe votes away from the incumbent.

Figure 5-2 presents an example of this strategy. A congressional incumbent was well known, but was worried about a major national trend running against his party. The campaign therefore decided to devote considerable resources to defining the challenger, who had been mayor of a local city and had approved several tax increases. The result was that although awareness of the challenger increased during the campaign, his unfavorables also steadily increased, so that by the end of October his ratio of favorable to unfavorable evaluations was not good. In short, this kind of preemptive campaign tries to limit the number of voters who are available to become swing voters.

Figure 5-2. Challenger's Favorable and Unfavorable Ratings in New York State Congressional Race

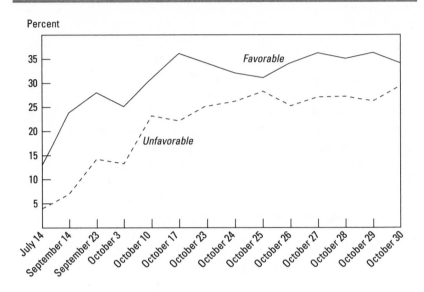

Superficial Awareness of Both Candidates

In some campaigns both candidates may be well known. In one mayor's race, for example, the incumbent Democratic mayor had battled with the Republican president of the city council for the four years preceding the election. As we tracked the name recognition and ratings of the likely candidates for the mayor's reelection campaign, it became clear that the Republican challenger was not going to start the formal race with a disadvantage in visibility and ratings. By May 1999 the candidates had very similar favorable and unfavorable ratings.

That same poll indicated that although both candidates had favorable images, most voters did not have much awareness of the records of the two candidates. Again, a lack of information was crucial to the race. Thus, a large percentage of the voters could probably be influenced by providing them with specific information about simple differences between the candidates, such as their positions on taxes or crime or a possible scandal in the housing office involving someone appointed by the mayor. That is, a large percentage of voters could probably be moved from one candidate to the other.

Faced with this situation—the mayor was particularly anxious that someone in the housing office would be indicted during the campaign—the mayor's campaign decided that it had to try to change the image of the Republican challenger. The campaign accordingly began a direct-mail campaign in which a positive piece about the mayor was followed by a negative piece about the challenger. The goal was to provide information about the challenger that would fill in her image and increase her negatives. The result was that her favorables stopped increasing and there was a very gradual increase in her negatives. The percentage of voters who might have been amenable to voting for the challenger was gradually reduced and the mayor was able to win by 15 percentage points.

Conclusion

A number of other chapters in this book have characterized swing voters as ambivalent or cross-pressured. Rather than seeing one candidate as clearly superior to the other, these voters see pluses and minuses in both candidates, in approximately equal proportions. Yet however well this description may apply to presidential elections, in subnational elections the archetypal swing voter is probably better described as *uninformed*. Not knowing very much at all about one or both candidates, many voters in state, congressional, or local elections are open to supporting either candidate, depending on which is better able to communicate a very modest level of information about his or her candidacy and positions.

There are, to be sure, uninformed voters who may not be swayed by information. Some incumbents are so highly regarded by and ideologically in sync with their constituencies that a challenger really has no chance of beating them, no matter how well known the challenger becomes. Other incumbents are potentially vulnerable because many voters have no idea what their record is, even if that vulnerability is not yet reflected in the polls. In a way that is still more art than science, a challenger must predict which voters are genuinely open to persuasion and whether there are enough of them to justify taking on an incumbent. Incumbents must take stock of their own liabilities and the strengths of potential challengers and then decide if there are preemptive strategies available that might prevent certain voters from ever getting to the point where they would seriously think about voting for the challenger. As I have tried to argue in this chapter, these sorts of questions are difficult to answer or even formulate in the abstract; analysts and strategists must take into account the specific context and circumstances of each campaign.

six

Swing Voters? Hah!
The Not Very "Persuadables" and the
Not Really "Undecideds" in 2004

Adam Clymer and Ken Winneg

Rarely if ever has the adage about "dancing with them that brung you" made more sense than in 2004. When the Bush and Kerry campaigns put most of their efforts into playing to their base voters, rather than trying to convert the uncommitted or the weak supporters of the other candidate, they knew what they were doing.

And when pollsters like us kept looking for something that would change an election that looked close all the way, we were—like stereotypical old generals—fighting a past war. This was not the traditional model, where candidates win nominations by playing to the left and the right and then win the general election by playing to the middle, where a decisive number of undecideds and weak supporters of the other candidate represent a valuable and winnable prize. Data from the National Annenberg Election Survey, a project of the Annenberg Public Policy Center of the University of Pennsylvania, make it clear that 2004 was a singularly stable election, one where voters may have had their doubts but hardly ever surrendered to them. Indeed, only 15 percent of voters said there was "ever a time" when they thought they would vote for the candidate other than the one they ultimately voted for.[1]

---

1. Data in this chapter are unweighted because of the difficulty in weighting a re-interviewed sample, and thus may differ slightly from some weighted data previously released by the National Annenberg Election Survey. But in those earlier releases, the differences between weighted and unweighted data rarely exceeded 1 percentage point.

The basic Annenberg survey interviewed 81,422 people between October 7, 2003, and November 16, 2004. The National Annenberg Election Survey (NAES), the nation's largest academic poll, uses a rolling cross-section methodology to measure when changes in candidate preference and voter knowledge occur and to understand campaign and news influences on the voters. The large size of the sample enables analysts to examine small groups of respondents—from American Indians to intended Bush voters who changed their minds—who cannot be studied with any accuracy in most polls.[2] In this chapter we focus on 7,050 respondents who were initially interviewed at some time before the election, and then were re-interviewed between November 4 and December 28, 2004. In that subsample, 3,433 people originally said they planned to vote for George W. Bush, and 3,333 said they planned to vote for John F. Kerry. Another 284 said they were undecided. When we re-interviewed them, 97.3 percent of the Bush backers said they stuck with him, as did 96.0 percent of the Kerry supporters.

But, of course, no one ever thought that most voters would be up for grabs. So at NAES, we looked for a segment of the population that could be moved. In some polls and media reports, and in the other chapters in this book, these folks are called swing voters. We did not use that term, however. The term *swing voters* is sometimes used to refer to people who vote for a Republican one year and a Democrat in another, or vice versa. Presumably such people exist, but we had no way to construct past voting histories of which we could be confident. Alternatively, the term *swing voter* sometimes refers to voters who go back and forth between candidates, perhaps several times, within one campaign, and we doubted that was what would happen in 2004. Instead we spoke of *persuadable voters,* a group we defined as including not only the openly undecided but also Bush or Kerry supporters who told us there was a "good chance" that they would change their preference, as distinguished from those who said they would "definitely" vote for their candidate or who said it was "pretty unlikely" that they would change (see box for exact question wordings).

The first thing to note about this group is that it wasn't very big, just 11.6 percent of the re-interviewed sample. The pure undecideds were the biggest segment of this group, at 4.7 percent. Another 3.7 percent backed Bush but said there was a "good chance" they could change their minds, and

2. The results and data from the 2000 survey were published in 2003 as *Capturing Campaign Dynamics: The National Annenberg Election Survey: Design, Method, and Data* (Romer and others 2003). The 2004 study was published in September 2006 (Romer and others 2006).

Wording of Vote-Preference and Strength-of-Support Questions in the National Annenberg Election Survey

1. Vote-preference question

Asked from March 3 to July 20, 2004
"If the 2004 presidential election were being held today, would you vote for George W. Bush, John Kerry, or Ralph Nader?" (The order of names was rotated.)

Asked after July 20, 2004
"If the 2004 presidential election were being held today, would you vote for George W. Bush and Dick Cheney, the Republicans; John Kerry and John Edwards, the Democrats; or Ralph Nader and Peter Camejo, of the Reform Party?" (The order of names was rotated.)

2. Strength-of-support question

"Will you definitely vote for George W. Bush/John Kerry/Ralph Nader for president, or is there a chance you could change your mind and vote for someone else?"

If respondent says could change mind: "Is there a good chance you'll change your mind or would you say it's pretty unlikely?"

3.2 percent said they preferred Kerry but there was a "good chance" that they would change their minds. Still, the election as a whole, and in several states in particular, was close enough so that if either side had won over far more of the other side's persuadables than it lost or had swept the undecideds while holding its own among the weakly committed, the results on November 2 could have been different.

But as it happened, not much persuasion occurred, even among the Bush or Kerry supporters who had said there was a "good chance" they might change their minds. Among the "persuadable" Bush supporters, 86.1 percent stayed with him, only marginally more than the 83.2 percent of "persuadable" Kerry voters who stayed with him. In comparison, among Bush supporters who said that they definitely would vote for him or that it was "pretty unlikely" they would switch, 98.3 percent stayed with Bush; in the comparable Kerry group, 96.9 percent stood by their man.

The later people in our persuadable grouping were interviewed, the more likely they were to change. To put it another way, if their commitment in October was still hedged, they were more likely to remain in play than if they had told us in July that they might switch. When we compared "persuadable" Bush backers who were first interviewed before October 1 with those interviewed later, we found that 88.1 percent of the early group stuck with Bush, compared

Figure 6-1. Percentage of "Persuadable" Voters during the 2004 Presidential Campaign: Five-Day Moving Average

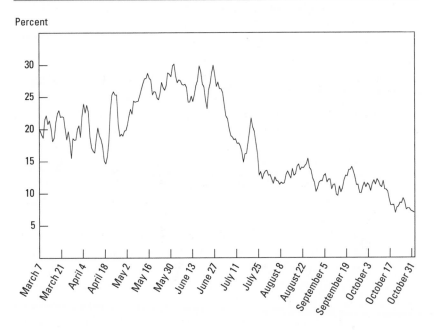

Source: National Annenburg Election Survey, 2004.

to 80.3 percent of the later group. Among Kerry "persuadables," there was slightly less difference, with 84.5 percent of the pre–October 1 respondents saying they stuck with him, compared to 78.8 percent of the later group.

These figures should be read against the ebb and flow of the size of the "persuadable" group. As figure 6-1 shows, the group began at around 20 percent in March and stayed between 25 and 30 percent from mid-May through the end of June, before declining steadily to about 15 percent in mid-July. It spiked up to 25 percent around the Democratic convention, staying between 10 and 15 percent until mid-October. By Election Day, it was around 7 percent.

The only group in which a substantial amount of persuasion occurred was the undecideds. (This was inevitable if they eventually decided to go ahead and vote for someone.) They divided almost evenly, with 46.8 percent for Bush and 46.4 percent for Kerry, 3 percent for Ralph Nader, and most of the rest scattered. An additional 3 percent, however, were never persuaded by anyone; they said they did not vote.

Against that background, let's go back to the Bush and Kerry supporters who said there was a "good chance" they would switch. Were there useful indicators that would suggest which of them were really available to be persuaded?

First, let us look at the "soft" Bush supporters. As noted, 86.1 percent of them voted for Bush—but 12.8 percent voted for Kerry. One indicator that distinguished these two groups was how they answered when asked to rate the two candidates on a favorability scale running from zero to ten. Among the 77.3 percent of "soft" Bush supporters who rated Bush higher than Kerry, 90.5 percent voted for him. If respondents rated the two candidates equally, as 16.5 percent did, Bush held on to three-quarters of them (75.6 percent). Bush even managed to win a slim majority (58.8 percent) of the small number of voters ($n = 17$) who rated Kerry higher. In short, Kerry had a better chance of winning over "soft" Bush supporters who rated Kerry as highly as or more highly than Bush than he did among those who had a more favorable view of Bush than of Kerry.

The same pattern emerged among the "soft" Kerry supporters. Nearly seven in ten (69.4 percent) rated Kerry more favorably than Bush. Among them, 88.7 percent stayed with Kerry. If they rated the two major-party candidates equally, as 21.8 percent of the "soft" Kerry supporters did, Kerry held on to 80.9 percent. But if they rated Bush higher than Kerry, as a small number did ($n = 19$), then the vote split evenly between Bush and Kerry, though the sample size is obviously too small to draw any firm conclusions about this group.

Preelection party identification was not a particularly useful indicator of how soft the "soft" supporters really were. Bush held on to 92 percent of the Republicans and 86.0 percent of the independents who said they supported him but that there was a "good chance" they would change their minds. Kerry retained 88.3 percent of his soft Democratic supporters and 85.2 percent of his soft independents. Weak crossover supporters, by contrast, really were weaker. Bush held on to only 66.7 percent of his soft Democratic backers and Kerry kept only 67.9 percent of his soft Republican supporters.

The foregoing suggests that very few of the soft supporters of either candidate were really persuadable, and that it might make more sense for pollsters to concentrate on the admittedly undecided, who made up just 4 percent of the sample. In fact, however, a lot of them may not have been as undecided as they claimed. Among the undecideds who gave Bush a higher rating than Kerry on the favorability scale, 84.2 percent voted for Bush. Among those who rated Kerry higher than Bush, 82.8 percent voted for Kerry. Using the relative favorabilities could put people who claim to be undecided in the proper column.

Does all this mean that we are doomed to a repetition of the turnout-based campaign of 2004, when the campaign discourse was dominated by partisan yammering and dishonest, fear-mongering attacks like the Republican National Committee's direct-mail charge that liberals like Kerry would ban the Bible or the Kerry campaign's claim that Bush planned to cut Social Security benefits by 30 to 45 percent? Perhaps. Minds were pretty well made up about Bush, pro or con, long before the 2004 campaign began. That freed the Republicans to spend their energies attacking Kerry rather than on the plans or achievements of their own candidate. Kerry tried to be positive about himself, but was continually drawn to playing to the Bush haters instead.

Things may be different in 2008 with the absence of a candidate as thoroughly defined as Bush. Although Hillary Clinton, if she is nominated, will almost certainly draw attacks designed to remind her severest critics why they cannot stand her, for all the candidates there will be another necessity. They will have to spend time and money discussing who they are and what they would like to do as president (not just how terrible the other candidates are). And that may leave voters truly undecided—and even persuadable—for months.

References

Romer, Daniel, and others. 2003. *Capturing Campaign Dynamics: The National Annenberg Election Survey: Design, Method, and Data.* Oxford University Press.
———. 2006. *Capturing Campaign Dynamics, 2000 and 2004: The National Annenberg Election Survey.* University of Pennsylvania Press.

seven
Do Swing Voters Swing Elections?

James E. Campbell

American presidential electoral politics are shaped to a great degree by two qualities: their competitiveness and their partisanship. American presidential politics are about as competitive as politics get. Even landslide presidential elections rarely reach a 60-40 split of the two-party vote, and most presidential elections are decided in the 55-to-45-percent range. American politics in general are also very partisan, and they have become more so in recent decades. Among those survey respondents who said that they voted (reported voters) in the 2004 election, about 40 percent identified strongly with either the Democratic or Republican parties and another 55 percent indicated some lesser level of party identification.[1] With competitive and highly partisan politics, it is natural that campaigns and those who observe them focus on the voters who are relatively uncertain about who they will vote for in an election. These potentially persuadable, or "up for grabs," voters have become known

---

1. These percentages were calculated from American National Election Study (ANES) data and have been corrected for the disparity between the vote division in the data and the actual national vote division. The proportion of strong party identifiers among reported voters in 2004 is very close to what it was in the 1950s and early 1960s, the heyday of modern partisanship as documented by the classic study of *The American Voter* (Campbell and others 1960). Those who are less identified with a political party include those who said that their identification was not very strong (about 29 percent in 2004) and those who initially said that they were independent but then said that they leaned toward a party (about 26 percent). Bruce E. Keith and his colleagues (1992) provide an array of evidence to indicate that these "leaners" are the equivalent of "not very strong" (often labeled "weak") partisans.

as swing voters. Not being firmly committed to vote for a particular candidate, these undecideds or persuadables may swing their votes toward one candidate or the other.

Politicians and political observers have long attempted to determine the characteristics of these swing voters in the hope that once they were identified, messages could be crafted to push or pull their decision one way or the other. In the late 1960s, Vice President Spiro Agnew talked about swing voters as the "silent majority."[2] Richard Scammon and Ben Wattenberg identified swing voters by the characteristics that they lacked: they were "unyoung, unpoor, unblack."[3] Later efforts to tag the elusive swing voters labeled them as Reagan Democrats, angry white men, soccer moms, NASCAR dads, security moms, and, most recently, mortgage moms.

The substantial attention devoted to swing voters is based, at least in part, on an implicit assumption that swing voters swing elections, that the votes of swing voters decide who wins presidential elections. The competitiveness of presidential elections and the partisanship of the electorate, providing many voters with a strong "standing decision" to vote for their party's standard bearer, make the importance of the swing vote a reasonable assumption. It is an especially reasonable assumption when the parties are relatively evenly balanced in partisans as they have been since the mid-1980s. It is quite likely that the median voter positioned to decide the election is also a swing voter. This does not mean, however, that most or even a majority of swing voters vote for the winning candidate or that the winning candidate requires a majority of the swing vote. It may be possible to win presidential elections with a large and activated base vote and only a small fraction of the swing vote.

The question posed in this chapter is whether winning presidential candidates in recent elections have carried or won a majority of the swing vote and whether they won *because* of the swing vote. If presidents are elected because of the swing vote, then the importance often attributed to swing voters by campaigns and the media is warranted. If, on the other hand, the swing vote has not been instrumental in electing presidents, then the role of the swing voter in the political landscape should be reassessed. If carrying the swing vote is not the key ingredient to a popular vote plurality, then how much of the swing vote do candidates need to win in order to achieve a popular vote victory?

2. Roberts and Hammond (2004, p. 313).
3. Scammon and Wattenberg (1971).

Who Are the Swing Voters?

In order to determine the impact of swing voters in deciding presidential elections, they must first be identified. What is distinctive about swing voters—what distinguishes them from nonswing voters—is that they are to some significant degree unsettled about how they will vote. It is clear that this is a matter of degree, that all voters are potentially open to changing their vote up until the moment it is cast. But voters differ in their degree of uncertainty about how they will vote, and some are much more open to being moved than others. At some level of this uncertainty, they can be labeled swing voters.

Three aspects of this vote uncertainty should be noted. First, the voter is not necessarily aware of or cognizant of his or her uncertainty about the vote choice. What makes a swing voter is the actual uncertainty of how the voter will vote and not whether the voter is subjectively willing to admit to this uncertainty. Many voters may harbor the illusion that they are open to either side in an election even though their vote choice is effectively well decided and predictable. Though voter-supplied information about the vote is useful in assessing the extent to which the vote choice is unsettled, saying you are a swing voter does not make you a swing voter. There must be a real possibility that your vote is moveable.

Second, at least for the purposes of this analysis, a swing voter is a voter. That is, swing voters are assumed to have turned out to vote. It is, of course, possible to include in the uncertainty about voting the decision of whether the potential voter will bother to vote. It would be understandable if many potential voters who are torn about whom to vote for decide not to vote. For the purposes of this analysis, these nonvoters were both potential voters and potential swing voters who, by opting not to vote, did not fulfill their potential.

Third, the uncertainty about how a voter will vote can (and most probably does) change over time. For instance, for many voters, their vote choice may be significantly less certain four or five months before the election than four or five weeks before the election. With more information and greater focus on that information, voters may become more settled in their vote for a candidate. It is, therefore, important to be time-specific in ascertaining who is and who is not a swing voter. In this analysis, given the limitations of available survey data, swing voters at two points in the election will be examined: precampaign swing voters and campaign swing voters. Precampaign swing voters are voters who we have reason to suspect are to a considerable degree uncertain in their vote choice well before the campaign begins. Their swing voter status is largely independent of the particular candidates running in the election. Campaign swing voters are voters who we have reason to suspect are to a considerable extent uncertain in their vote once the general election campaign is under way. These are swing voters who are unsettled in their vote after receiving information about the presidential candidates running in the particular election.

Who are the precampaign swing voters and how can they be best identified? The identification of precampaign swing voters draws on four different measures that have regularly been included in the American National Election Studies (ANES). First, precampaign swing voters are assumed not to be ideologically predisposed to vote for either of the major political parties' candidates. Since the 1972 election, the ANES has asked a national sample of potential voters what their ideological perspectives are. Using this measure, swing voters are assumed to be neither liberals, who are disposed to vote for the Democratic Party's presidential candidate, nor conservatives, who are disposed to vote for the Republican Party's presidential candidate. In other words, they are either moderates or people who are unable or unwilling to characterize their ideology. Second, among reported voters who are self-declared moderates or are unable or unwilling to describe their ideological perspective, precampaign swing voters are assumed not to be strongly identified with either political party. Third, among these reported voters who are moderates (or ideological "don't knows") without strong party identifications, precampaign swing voters are assumed not to be more supportive of one of the political parties than the median strong party identifier. The strength of a potential swing voter's relative affect for a political party is measured using "thermometer" scales, on which respondents are asked to rate their attitudes toward the political parties on a scale from zero (the maximum disaffection) to 100 degrees (the maximum affection). These questions are posed separately about the Democratic and Republican parties and then combined into a single hundred-point index (with 2 being the most pro-Republican score and 99 being the most pro-Democratic score). The median strong Republican since 1972 has had a score of 30 and the median strong Democrat has had a score of 70. Precampaign swing voters, then, must have a party thermometer index score of more than 30 but less than 70. Finally, respondents who reported that they had "known all along" how they would vote were classified as not being precampaign swing voters.

Who are the campaign swing voters? Two indicators in the ANES surveys were used to identify campaign swing voters. First, in every presidential election since 1952, ANES has asked potential voters to respond to a battery of four open-ended questions about what they like or dislike about each party's presidential candidate. Respondents may provide as many as five responses to each of the four questions. A simple count of these responses was found to be highly predictive of the reported vote choice.[4] The direction and intensity of a voter's preference can be measured by the sum of positive mentions ("likes") about the Democratic Party's candidate plus negative mentions ("dislikes") about the Republican Party's candidate minus the sum of positive mentions ("likes") about the Republican Party's candidate plus negative mentions ("dislikes") about the Democratic Party's candidate. This index ranges from positive 10 (the maximum preference for the Democratic candidate) to negative 10 (the maximum preference for the Republican candidate).

The second indicator used is the voter's party identification. This is meant to capture some unstated predispositions toward the candidates. Since the intensity of party identification is associated with loyalty rates in voting, strong Democrats are given a score of positive 2, weak and leaning Democrats positive 1, weak and leaning Republicans negative 1, and strong Republicans a score of negative 2. These party identification scores are added to the likes-dislikes measure to arrive at an index ranging from positive 12 (pro-Democrat) to negative 12 (pro-Republican).

An inspection of the predictive success of this index indicates that those scoring either 2 or over or negative 2 or under are very likely to vote for the preferred party's candidate. In elections since 1952, 93 percent of respondents scoring more than 1 on the index voted for the Democratic presidential candidate and 96 percent of respondents scoring less than negative 1 voted for the Republican presidential candidate. Those with scores of plus or minus 1 are much harder to predict. Only 66 percent of those with a score of 1 voted for the Democratic Party's presidential candidate, and 73 percent of those with a score of negative 1 voted for the Republican Party's standard bearer. The votes of those with a zero score have split nearly evenly, though with a slight Republican tilt (55 percent Republican to 45 percent Democratic). These voters with short-term evaluations (augmented by partisanship) near neutrality (negative 1, zero, or 1) are considered to be the campaign swing voters.

This likes-dislikes measure of the campaign swing vote corresponds fairly closely to the thermometer measure used by William G. Mayer in chapter 1 of this volume.[5] The underlying voter preference measures (before collapsing the measures to the simple dichotomous categories of swing and nonswing

4. Kelley and Mirer (1974); Kelley (1983).
5. All comparisons of the thermometer and likes-dislikes measures are based on reported voters for the major-party presidential candidates.

voters) are highly correlated. Over the ten elections since 1968 in which both measures are available, the median correlation between them was quite strong ($r = .84$).[6] Each measure was about equally and closely associated with the vote (median $r = .78$ for the thermometer measure and .77 for the likes-dislikes measure). In the typical election since 1968, both measures classified about 77 percent of the cases identically. This correspondence could have been even higher, but the cut-points selected by Mayer were more generous in classifying swing voters on the thermometer measure than the cut-points I used with the likes-dislikes measure. Mayer's coding typically counted an additional 8 percent of reported voters as swing voters (a median of 24 percent using Mayer's measure and cut-points as opposed to 16 percent using my measure and cut-points). Thus, even with identical underlying measures of vote preferences, the two counts would have had a disparity of 8 percentage points.[7] Overall, there appears to be a good degree of overlap between the measures, providing assurance that each is a credible basis for designating voter status as a swing or nonswing voter. While Mayer's thermometer measure is the simpler measure (whether the cut-points are tightened to plus or minus 10 thermometer points or left at 15 points), the likes-dislikes measure is used here because it is available over a longer series of elections. The likes-dislikes measure is available for every presidential election since 1952, whereas the thermometer measure cannot be constructed before the 1972 survey.[8]

How Many Voters Are Swing Voters?

Figure 7-1 displays the percentages of precampaign swing voters in each election since 1972 and campaign swing voters in each election since 1952. In all cases, ANES data have been weighted to reflect the actual division of the

6. Mayer's measure (see chapter 1, this volume) uses thermometer ratings from the pre-election survey; he therefore reports data only for the elections from 1972 to 2004. For 1968, I use the thermometer ratings from the postelection survey.

7. Using a 10-point (rather than 15-point) cut for Mayer's thermometer measure reduces the median percentage of swing voters from 24 to 19 percent. The median percentage of voters identically coded as swing or nonswing voters increases to 79 percent, using this tighter cut-point. The likes-dislikes and the thermometer counts of swing voters are very strongly correlated over time ($r = .75$, or .72 using the 15-thermometer-point coding). That is, both measures tend to identify the same years as having more or fewer swing voters.

8. An added virtue of the likes-dislikes measure is that it permits examination of the content of these swing voters' likes and dislikes. It might be helpful for campaigns to know whether swing voters were responding disproportionately to particular issues or candidate traits.

Figure 7-1. Swing Voters as a Percentage of Reported Voters, 1952–2004

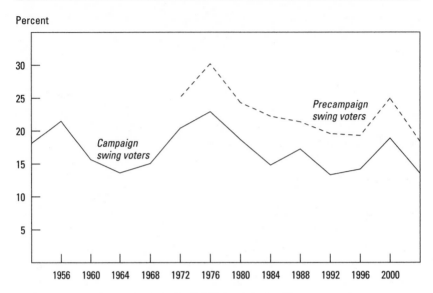

Percent

Source: American National Election Studies (ANES), Cumulative Data File.

national two-party vote. As is apparent from the figure, among reported voters, precampaign swing voters ranged from 18 to 30 percent with a median of 22 percent. Campaign swing voters ranged from 13 to 23 percent with a median of 16 percent. Put differently, the vote choice of roughly one out of every four or five voters is unsettled going into the typical campaign, and the vote choice of roughly one out of six voters remains unsettled during the typical campaign. In each election, as one might expect, the numbers of precampaign swing voters exceeded the numbers of campaign swing voters. The peaks of both precampaign and campaign swing voters appear to have occurred in the early 1970s during the depths of partisan dealignment and the transition to the new party system, and even though there has been a perceptible decline in swing voters over the last several elections, there were an unusual number of unsettled votes in the 2000 election between Al Gore and George W. Bush.

The numbers of swing voters are best appreciated when set in some perspective. First, in all elections, with respect to both precampaign and campaign swing voters, those who are settled in their vote choice substantially outnumber swing voters. In the typical election, the vote choices of nearly

80 percent of reported voters were largely settled before the campaign began, and nearly 85 percent were effectively settled once the campaign was under way. Second, there are more unsettled votes "in play" during a campaign than is suggested by most preference polls. Presidential preference polls rarely indicate an undecided vote of more than 4 to 6 percentage points. A more accurate portrait of the electorate would indicate three or four times as many unsettled votes. Third, with presidential elections typically decided by a vote margin of 4 to 5 percentage points (the winning two-party vote percentage over 50 percent), there are certainly enough swing voters to be decisive in the typical presidential election.

The Precampaign Swing Vote

Table 7-1 presents the analysis of the precampaign swing vote for the presidential candidate who received the majority of the national two-party popular vote. With the exception of the 2000 election, this is an analysis of the swing vote for the candidate who was elected to the presidency. The central question of interest is whether precampaign swing voters have determined which party's candidate won the majority of the popular vote. Though it is commonly assumed that carrying the swing vote is critical to winning a majority of the popular vote and with it the presidency, the evidence suggests otherwise.

The perception that carrying the precampaign swing vote is essential to a presidential victory may be due to the regularity with which the winning presidential candidate captures a majority of the swing vote. Seven of the nine presidential candidates since 1972 who received a majority of the popular vote also won a majority of the votes cast by precampaign swing voters. The only exceptions were the two most recent elections. In 2000, despite falling short of a popular-vote majority, George W. Bush rather than Al Gore narrowly carried a majority of the precampaign swing vote. In 2004, George W. Bush carried the popular vote but without a majority of the precampaign swing vote. Aside from these two cases, however, presidential candidates winning the overall vote also won the precampaign swing vote, and each of the nine majority-winning presidential candidates received at least 44.8 percent of the precampaign swing vote. In effect, if winning presidential candidates did not carry the precampaign swing vote outright, they came close to doing so.

Does the fact that winning presidential candidates usually captured the swing vote majority or came very close to doing so mean that the swing vote made these candidates the winners? With only one exception, the answer is no.

Table 7-1. The Precampaign Swing Vote, 1972–2004[a]

Percent

Election	Winning presidential party[b]	Swing voters as percentage of total vote[c]	Nonswing vote percentage for winner	Swing vote percentage for winner	Winner received a majority of the swing vote	Swing vote majority determined the winner	Swing vote percentage needed by the winner	Winning candidate needed a majority of the swing vote
1972	Republican	25.1	61.1	64.0	Yes	No	17.0	No
1976	Democrat	30.2	48.7	56.4	Yes	Yes	52.9	Yes
1980	Republican	24.3	51.2	67.9	Yes	No	46.1	No
1984	Republican	22.2	57.6	64.7	Yes	No	23.4	No
1988	Republican	21.4	53.3	56.3	Yes	No	38.0	No
1992	Democrat	19.6	52.2	58.6	Yes	No	40.9	No
1996	Democrat	19.3	53.0	62.1	Yes	No	37.6	No
2000	Democrat	25.0	51.3	47.0	No	No	46.0	No
2004	Republican	18.4	52.7	44.8	No	No	38.0	No

Source: American National Election Studies (ANES), Cumulative Data File.

a. Precampaign swing voters are reported voters in the ANES surveys who claimed to be moderate ideologically or responded "don't know" to the ideology question, were not strong party identifiers, indicated that they had not "known all along" how they would vote, and did not have a difference on the political party "thermometer items" more extreme than the median strong partisan. This last criterion meant that a voter could only be counted as a precampaign swing voter if he or she reported a major party thermometer index score between 30 and 70, where the index ranged from 2 (most pro–Republican Party) to 99 (most pro–Democratic Party).

b. The winning presidential party is the party whose candidate won a majority of the national two-party vote.

c. All vote percentages are of the two-party vote. The data are reweighted to conform to the actual two-party vote.

In eight of the nine elections examined, the winning presidential candidate had already carried a majority of the vote among voters who were *not* pre-campaign swing voters. In only one of the nine elections, the 1976 race between Gerald Ford and Jimmy Carter, did the swing vote majority override an opposite majority among nonswing voters. Those who were not precampaign swing voters gave Gerald Ford a narrow majority of their votes, while precampaign swing voters counteracted this by giving Jimmy Carter a 56 percent majority—but this was the only election in which the precampaign swing vote overrode the larger vote among nonswing voters.

Additional perspective on the importance of the precampaign swing vote to assembling a popular vote majority can be gained by determining what percentage of the precampaign swing vote the winning candidate needed in order to arrive at 50 percent of the two-party vote. Given the relative sizes of the precampaign swing vote and that portion of the electorate who were not precampaign swing voters, as well as the vote percentage (or proportion of the vote) that these nonswing voters provided to the winning candidate, some simple algebra allows us to calculate the percentage of the swing vote needed by each of the winning presidential candidates. These calculations are presented in the eighth column of table 7-1.

The results indicate that every winning presidential candidate since 1972 has needed at least 17 percent of the precampaign swing vote, but only Jimmy Carter in 1976 required a majority from precampaign swing voters in order to secure his popular vote majority. In general, the data indicate how little winning presidential candidates have depended upon the precampaign swing vote. Presidential candidates who won their elections by landslide proportions, such as Nixon in 1972 and Reagan in 1984, clearly did not need many swing votes to arrive at a majority. They had plenty of votes from everyone else. What is interesting is that presidential candidates winning with majorities well short of landslides also did not need to win a majority of the swing vote. The median winning presidential candidate in this period needed to attract only 38 percent of the precampaign swing vote in order to accumulate his popular vote majority. That is, the typical winning presidential candidate since 1972 could have lost the precampaign swing vote by a landslide and still won a majority of the national two-party popular vote. The notion that precampaign swing voters swing elections is a myth. Presidential candidates have not been able to win election without some portion of the precampaign swing vote, but most do not need more than two of every five swing voters.

The Campaign Swing Vote

Though only one recent presidential election has turned on who receives a majority of the precampaign swing vote, there remains the possibility that votes that appear unsettled during the campaign are more important to the election's outcome. Table 7-2 presents the analysis of the campaign swing vote. Unlike the precampaign swing vote analysis, the analysis of campaign swing votes covers the fourteen presidential elections since 1952. The analysis, though based on a different indicator of what constitutes a swing voter, in most respects supports the findings regarding precampaign swing voters.

As with the precampaign swing vote, winning presidential candidates usually received a majority of the campaign swing vote. The winning presidential candidate captured a majority of the campaign swing vote in ten of the fourteen elections since 1952. In three of the four elections in which the winning presidential candidate fell short of a swing vote majority (Eisenhower in 1956, Nixon in 1968, Carter in 1976, and Clinton in 1992), the winner attracted at least 46 percent of the swing vote. The winning presidential candidate with the lowest percentage of the campaign swing vote was Bill Clinton in 1992. With this exception, winning presidential candidates have done well among those unsettled about their vote during the campaign.

As with the precampaign vote, however, the success of winning presidential candidates among campaign swing voters does not mean that they won because of this success. Winning presidential candidates tend to do well among nonswing voters as well as swing voters. A majority of the campaign swing vote offset an opposing majority of the nonswing vote in only one of the fourteen presidential elections since 1952. That exception was the legendary 1960 election between Vice President Richard Nixon and Senator John Kennedy. Nixon narrowly carried the vote of the large number of settled, nonswing voters in the campaign whereas the campaign swing vote split nearly 55 percent to 45 percent in Kennedy's favor. Other than this one exception, the division of the swing vote either reinforced or merely muted the verdict of those who were settled in their votes early in the campaign.

The very limited impact of campaign swing voters is also evident from the calculations of what percentage of that vote winning candidates required in order to assemble their majorities (shown in the eighth column of table 7-2). In only one instance, the Kennedy-Nixon race of 1960, did the winning candidate need a majority of the campaign swing vote to capture his overall majority vote. Candidates who went on to win by landslides (Johnson in 1964, Nixon in 1972, and Reagan in 1984) did not need any or needed very few votes from campaign swing voters. Even setting aside these candidates, whose majorities were well settled before the campaign, the typical winning presidential candidate in this period was well enough supported that he required only about one-third of the campaign swing vote. Eisenhower in both 1952 and 1956, Reagan in 1980, and Clinton in both 1992 and 1996 required less than a third of the campaign swing vote to win their popular vote majorities. As with the precampaign swing vote, it is a myth that winning a majority of the campaign swing vote is necessary to win the presidential election. Most winning presidential candidates have been able to ride to victory with a minority of swing vote support.

The Impact of the Swing Vote

The analyses of both precampaign and campaign swing voters indicate that, contrary to conventional wisdom, presidential candidates do not need to carry a majority of the swing vote in order to win a majority of the two-party popular vote. Presidents have needed to pull some support from precampaign swing voters, but usually not very much. They have typically required less support, and in a few elections have needed no support, from campaign swing voters.

It is often thought that with both major-party candidates having a dependable base of partisan support and with elections being quite competitive, that the vote decisions of swing voters hold election outcomes in the balance. Apparently, this is not the case. The turnout and relative loyalties of the respective partisan bases have varied enough that they can effectively decide elections with only the help of a relatively small share of the swing vote.

Although this finding deflates the conventional wisdom's claims of the importance of swing voters, it is nothing new—it is consistent with a substantial body of electoral research over the years. Paul Lazarsfeld, a coauthor of both *The People's Choice* and *Voting*, two landmark studies in the field of electoral research, wrote in the 1940s that "in an important sense, modern Presidential campaigns are over before they begin."[9] It is not that campaigns have no impact, according to Lazarsfeld, but that (in the age before digital photography) campaigns are "like the chemical bath which develops a photograph. The chemical influence is necessary to bring out the picture, but only the picture pre-structured on the plate can come out."[10] This perspective

9. Lazarsfeld, Berelson, and Gaudet (1944); Berelson, Lazarsfeld, and McPhee (1954); Lazarsfeld (1944, p. 317).
10. Lazarsfeld (1944, p. 330).

Table 7-2. The Campaign Swing Vote, 1952–2004[a]

Percent

Election	Winning presidential party[b]	Swing voters as percentage of total vote[c]	Nonswing vote percentage for winner	Swing vote percentage for winner	Winner received a majority of the swing vote	Swing vote majority determined the winner	Swing vote percentage needed by the winner	Winning candidate needed a majority of the swing vote
1952	Republican	18.1	54.5	59.1	Yes	No	29.9	No
1956	Republican	21.5	60.4	48.1	No	No	11.9	No
1960	Democrat	15.7	49.2	54.9	Yes	Yes	54.3	Yes
1964	Democrat	13.6	62.8	52.1	Yes	No	0.0	No
1968	Republican	15.1	50.6	49.2	No	No	46.5	No
1972	Republican	20.4	62.9	57.6	Yes	No	0.0	No
1976	Democrat	22.9	52.2	46.0	No	No	41.4	No
1980	Republican	18.7	55.2	55.9	Yes	No	27.5	No
1984	Republican	14.8	57.2	70.8	Yes	No	8.9	No
1988	Republican	17.3	53.4	56.3	Yes	No	33.7	No
1992	Democrat	13.3	55.2	41.9	No	No	16.0	No
1996	Democrat	14.2	53.8	60.5	Yes	No	27.2	No
2000	Democrat	18.9	50.3	50.3	Yes	No	48.9	No
2004	Republican	13.5	50.6	55.5	Yes	No	46.3	No

Source: American National Election Studies (ANES), Cumulative Data File.

a. Campaign swing voters are calculated using the ANES questions about voter likes and dislikes about the presidential candidates and the voter's party identification. Each mention of a like for a party is counted for it and a dislike counted against it. An identification for a party is counted in its favor and a strong identification is counted further to its credit. The total of these counts can range from +12 in favor of the Democrats to –12 in favor of the Republicans. Those with scores of (–1, 0, or +1 are classified as campaign swing voters.

b. The winning presidential party is the party whose candidate won a majority of the national two-party vote.

c. All vote percentages are of the two-party vote. The data are reweighted to conform to the actual two-party vote.

may exaggerate the fixed nature of public opinion and underestimate the potential for vote shifts, but it is not far off the mark in suggesting that most of the fundamental influences on elections are in place well before the campaign begins.

The belief that presidential elections are often effectively decided before the general election campaigns begin to settle the vote choices of swing voters is not confined to academic students of elections. James Farley, Franklin Roosevelt's campaign manager in his 1932 and 1936 presidential victories, promulgated "Farley's Law": that presidential elections were decided before rather than after Labor Day of the election year.[11]

The marginal character of the importance of swing voters to presidential elections is also consistent with the findings of the National Election Studies that typically two-thirds of voters say they decided how they would vote at or before the national nominating conventions in the summer of the election year.[12] It is also consistent with the marginal impact of the independent vote on presidential elections; late deciding voters splitting evenly between the major-party candidates with a tilt toward returning to vote for their party's standard bearer; the greater importance of precampaign party unity to the election results; the importance of precampaign fundamentals to the accuracy of election forecasts; and the infrequency with which campaign effects have decided which party has won the presidency.[13]

Given the abundance of evidence indicating that swing voters (or late deciders, preference changers, and independents) have a very limited impact on presidential elections, why do they receive the enormous attention that they do? One reason may be the democratic belief that elections should not be decided until voters go into the polling booth to cast their ballots, that voters should keep open minds and listen to all that the candidates have to say before they reach a final decision. Journalists, political junkies, and supporters of trailing candidates also want to keep the election story alive (or to keep hope alive), and elevating the role of the swing voter is one way to do so. Finally, the history of both precampaign swing voters and campaign swing voters is that they each made a critical difference in at least one election. Precampaign swing voters were responsible for electing Jimmy Carter in 1976 and campaign swing voters were responsible for electing John Kennedy in

11. Troy (1996, p. 191); Faber (1965, p. 186).
12. Campbell (2000, table 1.2).
13. Campbell (2000, table 4.1; 2001a; 2007; 2005; 2001b).

1960. There is always the possibility that swing voters could make a critical difference in the next election, but if history is a guide, the odds are that they will not decide the election.

References

Berelson, Bernard R., Paul F. Lazarsfeld, and William N. McPhee. 1954. *Voting.* University of Chicago Press.

Campbell, Angus, Philip E. Converse, Warren E. Miller, and Donald E. Stokes. 1960. *The American Voter.* New York: Wiley.

Campbell, James E. 2000. *The American Campaign: U.S. Presidential Campaigns and the National Vote.* Texas A&M University Press.

———. 2001a. "Presidential Election Campaigns and Partisanship." In *American Political Parties: Decline or Resurgence?,* edited by Jeffrey E. Cohen, Richard Fleisher, and Paul Kantor, pp. 11–29. Washington: CQ Press.

———. 2001b. "When Have Presidential Campaigns Decided Election Outcomes?" *American Politics Research* 29, no. 5: 437–60.

———. 2005. "The Fundamentals in U.S. Presidential Elections: Public Opinion, the Economy, and Incumbency in the 2004 Presidential Election." *Journal of Elections, Public Opinion and Parties* 15, no. 1: 73–83.

———. 2007. "Nomination Politics, Party Unity, and Presidential Elections." In *Understanding the Presidency,* edited by James P. Pfiffner and Roger H. Davidson, pp. 74–90. 4th ed. New York: Pearson Longman.

Faber, Harold. 1965. *The Road to the White House.* New York: New York Times.

Keith, Bruce E., David B. Magleby, Candice J. Nelson, Elizabeth Orr, Mark C. Westlye, and Raymond E. Wolfinger. 1992. *The Myth of the Independent Voter.* University of California Press.

Kelley, Stanley, Jr. 1983. *Interpreting Elections.* Princeton University Press.

Kelley, Stanley, Jr., and Thad W. Mirer. 1974. "The Simple Act of Voting." *American Political Science Review* 68, no. 2: 572–91.

Lazarsfeld, Paul F., 1944. "The Election Is Over." *Public Opinion Quarterly* 8, no. 3: 317–30.

Lazarsfeld, Paul F., Bernard Berelson, and Hazel Gaudet. 1944. *The People's Choice.* New York: Duell, Sloan & Pearce.

Roberts, Robert North, and Scott John Hammond. 2004. *Encyclopedia of Presidential Campaigns: Slogans, Issues, and Platforms.* Westport, Conn.: Greenwood.

Scammon, Richard M., and Ben J. Wattenberg. 1971. *The Real Majority.* New York: Coward, McCann & Geoghegan.

Troy, Gil. 1996. *See How They Ran.* Rev. ed. Harvard University Press.

eight
Conclusion:
The State of the Discussion

William G. Mayer and Ruy Teixeira

The first word on a subject is never the last word. The conference on swing voters that took place at Northeastern University in mid-2006 was not organized with the intention of achieving or imposing an early and premature consensus. On the contrary, we deliberately tried to invite a diverse array of participants, united only by the fact that they had done research (or, in some cases, could be persuaded to do research) on swing voters. In this final chapter, then, we want to sum up the state of the discussion: What things do the contributors to this volume appear to agree about, what do they disagree about, what work remains to be done?

These points of agreement and disagreement are discussed in detail in this chapter, but it is worth stressing the extent to which the research reported in this volume challenges the current conventional wisdom on swing voters. For example, one point of agreement is that the demographic differences between swing and nonswing voters are typically modest, suggesting that the media obsession with demographically defined swing voter groups (soccer moms, office park dads, and so forth) is ill advised. Nor is there much evidence at this point that swing voters have similar interests in policy terms, despite the strenuous efforts of commentators and consultants to impute a distinct viewpoint to these voters. As for the importance of swing voters to election outcomes, it appears that those who seek a clear answer on one side (swing voters always decide elections!) or the other (it's all about mobilizing the base!) will be disappointed. Reality, as we outline below, is considerably more complicated.

What Is a Swing Voter?

To begin with the most basic point, the authors of the chapters in this book do seem to agree on the fundamental question of definition. Swing voters are voters who are "relatively uncertain about who they will vote for in an election . . . [voters who are] potentially persuadable or 'up for grabs'" (chapter 7); voters who have "not developed a committed preference for one candidate" (chapter 3); voters whose "preferences might be influenced by the campaign" (chapter 4); voters who are "undecided" or express "a less-than-firm commitment to their candidate" (chapter 2). Adam Clymer and Ken Winneg (chapter 6) call them "persuadable voters."

Identifying Swing Voters in Sample Surveys

How can swing voters be identified in surveys of the mass electorate? The authors assembled here use three major approaches to operationalize the swing voter concept.

All of the public pollsters—Annenberg, Gallup, and Pew—began by asking voters, in the now-familiar way, which candidate they would vote for "if the election were held today." All those who were undecided were classified as swing voters.[1] All three organizations then posed a follow-up question that straightforwardly asked voters whether they might "change their mind" or whether there was any chance they might vote for the opposing candidate. Those who indicated that there was a reasonable chance they would change their vote were also put in the swing voter category. To facilitate comparison, the swing voter questions that each survey organization used in 2004 are listed in the box.

A second approach was employed by James E. Campbell and William G. Mayer, both of whom used data from the American National Election Studies (ANES) to create a graduated scale that measured a voter's comparative assessment of the two major-party presidential candidates.[2] Those in the cen-

1. Gallup and Pew asked all undecided voters a follow-up question about whether they "leaned" toward one of the candidates. All leaners were also classified as swing voters. Annenberg did not include such a question in its surveys because they "were never planning to publish 'horserace' [figures] and felt it unnecessary to 'push' the undecideds" (Ken Winneg, personal communication to the authors, June 25, 2007).

2. Unfortunately, ANES has never included a question similar to the ones listed in the box, so it is impossible to compare how closely Mayer or Campbell's measure overlaps with the

Questions Used by the Annenberg, Gallup, and Pew Surveys to Identify Swing Voters in 2004

Annenberg

"Will you definitely vote for [preferred presidential candidate] for president, or is there a chance you could change your mind and vote for someone else?" If respondent says could change mind: "Is there a good chance you'll change your mind or would you say it's pretty unlikely?"

Only respondents who said there was a "good chance" they would change their minds were classified as swing voters.

Gallup

"Are you certain now that you will vote for [preferred presidential candidate] for president, or do you think you may change your mind between now and the November election?"

"Is there any chance you will vote for [other major presidential candidate] in November or is there no chance whatsoever that you will vote for him?"

Gallup asked both questions in 2004, but predominantly the first.

Pew

If respondent expressed intention to vote for Bush: "Do you think there is a chance that you might vote for John Kerry in November, or have you definitely decided not to vote for him?"

If respondent expressed intention to vote for Kerry: "Do you think there is a chance that you might vote for George Bush in November, or have you definitely decided not to vote for him?"

---

ter of this scale—respondents who rated the candidates equal or almost equal—were classified as swing voters.

Finally, Daron R. Shaw identified swing voters on the basis of their voting histories. The underlying idea here was that each voter has "a probability of voting for a particular party in a generic election"—a probability that is best measured by observing how he or she has voted in past elections. Using panel data from the ANES that allowed him to examine an individual voter's behavior over three consecutive presidential elections, Shaw defined swing voters as

---

Annenberg, Gallup, or Pew results. After the standard presidential vote question, ANES does ask respondents whether their "preference for this candidate is strong or not strong," but as Jones demonstrates in chapter 2, this type of question is not a very good measure of what it means to be a swing voter.

those who had shown some variation in their voting: who had either voted for presidential candidates from two different parties or who had not voted at all in one or two of the three elections.

The identification of swing voters can also be a significant matter in subnational elections. As Jeffrey Stonecash points out in chapter 5, however, most attempts to identify swing voters assume that voters have at least a minimum level of information about both major candidates. This assumption applies quite well to a presidential general election but is almost certainly not an accurate description of the state of voter knowledge in most subnational elections. Mayer's attempt to construct a swing voter scale out of the ANES thermometer ratings is particularly guilty on this score, since it requires every respondent to provide some kind of rating for *both* major-party presidential candidates. (Those who say they don't know how to rate one of the candidates are treated as missing data.) In presidential elections, only a very tiny percentage of voters—about 1 percent, on average—are unable to meet this standard, but the number is far higher in congressional elections. In a similar way, to take voters at their word when they say that they are voting for Bush and that there is no chance they will change their minds assumes that the voters know enough about both Bush and Kerry to make such an assertion meaningful. In nonpresidential elections, as Stonecash shows, identifying swing voters is a much more difficult enterprise, at times requiring the analyst to make some assumptions about how voters might respond if they were to become aware of certain kinds of information. In some state or local elections with no incumbent, almost everybody in the electorate may reasonably be described as a swing voter—open to voting for either candidate, depending on how much and what they learn during the campaign.

The Size of the Swing Vote

What percentage of the electorate are swing voters? Even if we restrict our attention to presidential elections, this is a very difficult question to answer in general terms. The size of the swing voter pool depends on the election year, the survey questions used to identify them, and the point in the election cycle at which a survey is conducted. With regard to the last of these factors, the 2004 Annenberg study provides a particularly good venue for observing the fluctuations in the size of the swing voter group over a single election year. Starting at about 20 percent of the likely electorate in March, the number of swing voters rose to around 30 percent in May and June, dropped to about 15 percent after the Democratic National Convention, and then declined

Table 8-1. Annenberg, Gallup, and Pew Estimates of the Percentage of Swing Voters in 2004

Percent

Period	Annenberg	Gallup	Pew
September through mid-October[a]	10–15	13–19	19–24
Election eve	7	11	19

a. All three organizations took multiple readings during this period. Figures are the lowest and highest reported estimates.

slowly to 7 percent in the final preelection survey. The Gallup Poll, which has been asking various types of swing voter questions since the 1940s, has also found that the percentage of swing voters "usually" declines over the course of the campaign—but not always. "In 1988 and 1996, the proportion held fairly steady throughout, and in 1992 and to a lesser extent in 2000 it increased later in the campaign," according to Jeffrey M. Jones (chapter 2, this volume).

With this caveat in mind, we can compare the Annenberg, Gallup, and Pew estimates of the percentage of swing voters at two points during the 2004 campaign (table 8-1): September through mid-October, and just before the election. Obviously there is some measure of variation in both sets of estimates. The Annenberg figures are consistently lower than those produced by the other two organizations, probably because Annenberg uses a two-question sequence to identify swing voters and does not include in that category all voters who say they could change their minds but only those who say there is a "good chance" that they will do so. For less obvious reasons, the Pew estimates are consistently larger than the Annenberg and Gallup numbers.

If the three surveys do not exactly coincide, however, they may at least be said to be "in the same ballpark." As James Campbell correctly notes in chapter 7, what distinguishes swing voters from nonswing voters is "a matter of degree": ". . . all voters are potentially open to changing their vote up until the moment it is cast. But voters differ in their degree of uncertainty about how they will vote, and some are much more open to being moved than others. At some level of this uncertainty, they can be labeled swing voters." Given the inherent "squishiness" of the category, and given the lack of previous research on the topic, it is, we think, striking that the three organizations came as close to one another as they did. In particular, all three polls show that swing voters are a distinct minority of the total electorate, though certainly large enough to make the difference in a close election.

Table 8-2. Mayer's and Campbell's Estimates of the Percentage of Swing Voters, 1972–2004

Percent

Year	Mayer	Campbell
1972	22	20
1976	34	23
1980	28	19
1984	22	15
1988	26	17
1992	22	13
1996	18	14
2000	23	19
2004	13	13
Average	23	17
Standard deviation	5.9	3.5

As previously noted, the size of the swing voter population also varies from one election to another. Table 8-2 shows Mayer and Campbell's estimates of the proportion of swing voters for every presidential election between 1972 and 2004. Though Mayer's figures are both higher and more variable than Campbell's, the two sets of numbers are highly correlated ($r = .80$). Both show that swing voters were relatively plentiful in the elections of 1972 to 1980.

Of more immediate interest is the fact that both studies show the 2004 election to have been a contest in which the proportion of swing voters was unusually small. Mayer's data provide particularly striking evidence on this point: just 13 percent of the 2004 voters were swing voters, as compared to a 1972-2004 average of 23 percent. Chapters 2 and 4 of this volume reach the same conclusion. Examining a Gallup swing voter question that was asked from 1992 to 2004, Jones notes that at least 40 percent of registered voters were swing voters during the spring and summer of 1992 and 1996, versus 29 percent in 2000 and 20 percent in 2004. Shaw similarly found that whereas 44 percent of the electorate were swing voters from 1968 to 1976, just 24 percent fit this description in presidential elections from 1996 to 2004.

The Distinctiveness of Swing Voters

Given the diversity of approaches that various authors use to identify swing voters, there is a striking measure of agreement about a number of other empirical findings. First, swing voters do have a number of distinctive *attitudinal* characteristics that set them apart from the rest of the electorate. Mayer (chapter 1), Jones (chapter 2), and Michael Dimock, April Clark, and Juliana Menasce Horowitz (chapter 3) all found that swing voters were substantially less partisan and more moderate than nonswing voters.

The same three chapters also provide evidence showing that swing voters are less engaged in politics than those who have reached a firm decision about which candidate to support. At one level this finding underlines a central difficulty of contemporary American election campaigns: if a candidate makes a speech, runs an ad, or participates in a debate, the people who are most likely to notice it are those who have already made up their minds. By contrast, the people who need the information most are least likely to come in contact with it. Yet swing voters are not so isolated or apolitical as to make the campaigner's task impossible. As Dimock, Clark, and Horowitz conclude, swing voters are probably best characterized as a "middle-awareness group." They do not follow the campaign as closely as committed voters do, but they are not as disengaged as nonvoters are.

Swing voters are not particularly distinctive demographically, however. As Shaw concludes, "Individual psychological factors are significantly more important for explaining swing voting than being a member of a particular group." Though media stories often try to portray swing voters as consisting disproportionately of one or a small number of demographic groups (typical candidates include women, Latinos, and suburbanites), the data provide strikingly little support for such claims. On most demographic measures, the differences between swing voters and the rest of the electorate are small and statistically insignificant. Where differences do exist, moreover, they vary from election to election: a group that is overrepresented among swing voters in one year will generally not be so positioned in subsequent years. In demographic terms, the most prominent characteristic of swing voters is their diversity.

One major topic that has not been adequately addressed in these chapters, and therefore should be tagged as a subject for further research, is whether swing voters differ from nonswing voters in the *direction* of their issue opinions. Besides being more moderate, are swing voters, at least in some years, more in favor of universal health care or less in favor of abortion? Although chapter 2 touches briefly on this issue, none of the authors gives this matter the sustained analysis it deserves.

Swing Voters and Election Outcomes

The authors in this volume are less in agreement as to how important the swing vote has actually been in recent presidential elections. Mayer argues that except in a small number of landslide elections, the "base vote" for most presidential candidates—what other authors in this book call the "committed voters"—falls well short of a majority of the two-party popular vote. The critical margin of victory for most presidential candidates is thus provided by swing voters. James Campbell, looking at the same data, finds that swing voters rarely cast their ballots in a way that diverges radically from the rest of the electorate. While winning presidential candidates tend to do well among swing voters, they also fare well among nonswing voters. Indeed, of the fourteen presidential elections Campbell analyzes, in only one instance, 1960, did a majority of swing voters offset an opposing majority of nonswing voters. In other years, says Campbell, "The division of the swing vote either reinforced or merely muted the verdict of those who were settled in their votes early in the campaign."

Are Swing Voters Really Worth All the Trouble?

Finally, are swing voters really worth all the attention that has been lavished on them in recent elections? Here, too, there is a divergence of opinion. On the one hand, there was impressive evidence, in virtually every chapter, that even weak and halfhearted candidate preferences can be quite powerful. Annenberg, Pew, and Gallup all found that, of swing voters who expressed a mild preference for one candidate over the other, the overwhelming majority stayed with that candidate through all the ups and downs of the campaign and then finally voted for him on Election Day. Similarly, Mayer's analysis (chapter 1) showed that if respondents rated one candidate just 10 degrees higher than the other in the preelection poll, at least 80 percent would end up voting for that higher-rated candidate.

So why do campaigns target swing voters? Probably the best answer to this question is: What's the alternative? If many swing voters are, in fact, not very easy to persuade, committed voters are even more immovable. Clymer and Winneg found that of those Bush supporters who said there was a "good chance" they might change their minds, 86 percent didn't change their minds and ultimately voted for Bush. But among the "unpersuadable" Bush supporters—those who said they would definitely vote for him or that it was "pretty unlikely" they would switch—the loyalty rate was even higher: 98 percent stuck with the incumbent president.

Some readers will say that there *is* another alternative. Given how difficult it is to convert the weakly committed or to win an overwhelming majority of the truly undecided, perhaps presidential campaigns would be better advised to do what the Bush campaign did in 2004: ignore (or at least don't place much emphasis on) the swing voters and try instead to mobilize the committed voters. Since there is little doubt that this strategy will get a great deal of attention in the 2008 elections, two general points should be made about it. The first is that persuading the swing voters and mobilizing the already committed are not necessarily incompatible or mutually exclusive strategies. Historically, most campaigns have tried, at least to some degree, to do both. For example, the 2004 Bush campaign did devote a good deal of time and effort to getting out the vote on Election Day, but it also spent millions of dollars on ads that were plainly designed to sway the uncommitted.[3]

Second, since many chapters in this book have emphasized the difficulties of converting the swing voters, it is important to state that mobilizing non-voters is also a difficult undertaking. Over the last several decades, strategists and commentators on both the left and the right have periodically claimed that there are large numbers of Americans currently on the political sidelines who would love to vote if only one of the parties would make a real effort to reach out to them. American turnout rates are held down, according to this argument, because both the Democrats and Republicans are afraid they would lose control of a system suddenly inundated by millions of fractious, new, antiestablishment voters. Well, it sounds nice, but there is little evidence to support this claim. Nonvoters are distinguished chiefly by their lack of interest in and attention to politics. They are neither closet liberals nor closet conservatives. If there really were some kind of "magic bullet"—a particular tactic or set of issue appeals that would mobilize huge numbers of previous nonvoters—surely some candidate running for president or governor or senator would have found it by now, and once other candidates saw how successful it was, it would have been widely copied and imitated until it became standard practice. In fact, year in and year out, national turnout in presidential elections hovers between 50 and 60 percent, while midterm turnout rates bounce around between 35 and 45 percent.

Of all the things under the control of campaigns,[4] the only one that has been clearly shown to have a substantial effect on voter turnout is door-to-

---

3. Certainly this was true in Ohio, where it is, in fact, difficult to make the case that mobilization alone was the key to Bush's crucial win in that state. Turnout actually went up more in heavily Democratic areas than in heavily Republican areas in Ohio in 2004, suggesting that voter persuasion played a key role in Bush's narrow victory in that state, despite media coverage that stressed only Republican mobilization efforts.

4. This qualification is important. There may be a number of things that the state or federal government can do to increase turnout, such as adopting Election Day registration

door canvassing. As Donald Green and Alan Gerber conclude after a careful review of the experimental evidence, "As a rule of thumb, one additional vote is produced for every fourteen people who are successfully contacted by canvassers."[5] Yet however encouraging this finding might initially appear to be, it actually speaks more eloquently about the limitations of mobilization strategies. A comprehensive door-to-door canvass may be an efficient and manageable objective for someone running for city council or state representative, but it is very difficult to implement in a large constituency. In a statewide race, for example, it requires a campaign to find thousands of volunteers or paid canvassers, in widely scattered locations, and then to supervise and coordinate their efforts. Door-to-door canvassing is also hard to monitor: local canvassers and field coordinators often make exaggerated reports about the work being done, reports that the higher-ups at campaign headquarters generally find difficult to challenge or disprove. Finally, Green and Gerber's finding that canvassing produces one additional vote "for every fourteen people *who are successfully contacted*" (emphasis added) needs to be taken in conjunction with their discussion about the difficulties of contacting many people because they aren't home or refuse to open the door or because the canvasser cannot gain access to an apartment building or gated community. In most of the experiments they report, the contact rate—the proportion of people in the treatment group who lived in a household where at least one person was contacted by a canvasser—was typically about 30 percent.[6] It is precisely these problems that explain why modern campaigns often omit or downplay door-to-door canvassing and use phone calls or direct mail to mobilize their supporters on Election Day—two forms of get-out-the-vote activity that require less lead time and manpower and are easier to monitor. Unfortunately, according to Green and Gerber, direct mail and phone banks have much weaker and inconsistent effects on turnout.

There is, in short, no compelling reason to think that mobilizing committed voters is a more effective strategy than trying to persuade swing voters. Even in the polarized politics of the early twenty-first century, it is likely that almost all campaigns will try to do both.

(though the efficacy of many such reforms is also widely disputed). But this knowledge is of no help to a candidate in the middle of an election campaign.

5. D. P. Green and A. S. Gerber, *Get Out the Vote! How to Increase Voter Turnout* (Brookings, 2004, p. 34).

6. Green and Gerber, appendix A.

Contributors

James E. Campbell
University at Buffalo SUNY

April Clark
*Pew Research Center for the People
and the Press*

Adam Clymer
*Annenberg Public Policy Center,
University of Pennsylvania*

Michael Dimock
*Pew Research Center for the People
and the Press*

Juliana Menasce Horowitz
*Pew Research Center for the People
and the Press*

Jeffrey M. Jones
The Gallup Poll

William G. Mayer
Northeastern University

Daron R. Shaw
University of Texas–Austin

Jeffrey M. Stonecash
Syracuse University

Ruy Teixeira
Center for American Progress and
The Century Foundation

Ken Winneg
*Annenberg Public Policy Center,
University of Pennsylvania*

Index

African Americans: and party identification, 25, 89, 90, 97; as swing voters,
26, 51, 94, 95, 119. *See also* Racial
preferences
Aggregate-level conception of swing
voting, 87, 98
Agnew, Spiro, 119
American National Election Studies
(ANES), 5–9; and demographic
stability, 27; and frequency of swing
voting, 76; ideology measurement in,
23–24; and marginal voters, 17, 18;
party identification question, 10;
preelection surveys, 20, 22, 121; and
timing of voter commitment to
candidate, 131; and undecided vote,
14, 16, 81–82, 83; and vote choice
stability, 86, 87–88; weighting data
from, 19, 123–24. *See also* Presidential
elections
The American Voter (Campbell and
others), 59, 76–77
Anderson, John, 42

ANES. *See* American National Election
Studies
Annenberg surveys. *See* National
Annenberg Election Survey (NAES)
"Any chance/no chance" question, 48–50,
57

Base vote by party, 19–21, 29, 97, 112, 119
Battleground states, 4
Berelson, Bernard, 59, 76
Binning, William, 9
Blacks. *See* African Americans; Racial
preferences
Blumenthal, Mark, 80–81
Bowers, Chris, 79
Boyd, Richard, 85
Buchanan, Pat, 48
Bush, George H. W., 15, 21, 22, 43, 46–47
Bush, George W.: in *2000* election, 49–50,
56, 92, 98, 124, 125; in *2004* election,
48–49, 54, 82, 98, 112–17; approval
rating, 108–09; and base vote, 21; and
campaign issues, 65; and

Easterly, Larry, 9
Educational levels of voters, 62, 89, 90, 94, 96, 97
Edwards, John, 60
Eisenhower, Dwight, 37, 82, 128, 129
Elderly as swing voters, 26, 51, 64, 89, 94, 95
Election outcomes, 19–22, 69–70, 71, 118–32. *See also* Power of swing voters
Electoral College, 4
Elmira, New York, studies, 76
Erie County, Ohio, studies, 76
Evolution of swing voters, 54–56, 120

Farley, James, 131
Favorable view of candidates: in *2004* election, 53, 72–73, 116; measurements of, 121–23; and strength-of-support question, 57; in subnational campaigns, 104, 109; and trends in election years, 53; and undecided voters, 84
"Feeling thermometer" questions. *See* Thermometer ratings
Floating voters. *See* Party switchers
Ford, Gerald, 28, 40, 127; pardon of Nixon, 13
Future research suggestions, 29–30, 139

Gallup, George, 32
Gallup Poll (*1944–2004*), 32–57; and candidate preferences, 78, 103, 134, 135; contemporary history of, 44–50; and demographic characteristics of swing voters, 50–51, 52, 57; and final vote projections, 80; and issue differences, 54; *1972–88* history of, 39–44; and nonvoters, 55–56; and number of swing voters, 56, 137; and political characteristics of swing voters, 51–54, 57; postelection panel studies, 54–56; pre-*1972* history of, 33–39; and undecided voters, 15, 22, 83, 134, 135, 140; wording of, 34–38, 57, 135

Gaudet, H., 76
Gelman, Andrew, 15
Gerber, Alan, 142–43
Get-out-the-vote activity, 78, 129, 141, 142
Goldwater, Barry, 38, 82
Gore, Al, 20, 48, 124, 125
Green, Donald, 142–43
Group identities. *See* Aggregate-level conception of swing voting; Demographic characteristics of swing voters

Health care as issue, 54
"Heuristics," 60
"Hidden partisans," 10
High-income voters. *See* Income levels of voters
Hispanics as swing voters, 26, 89, 94, 96, 98, 139
Holbrook, Thomas, 59
Horowitz, Juliana Menasce, 58–74, 139
Humphrey, Herbert, 82

Identification of swing voters: and campaign dynamics, 60–64; distinguishing from other voters, 22–26; and election outcomes, 120–23; in Gallup polls, 50–54; in low information elections, 103–10; major approaches to, 134–36; and presidential elections, 60–64, 93–97
Ideology and labels, 23–24, 63–64, 77, 86–87, 89, 121
Ignoring swing voters, as campaign strategy, 141
Income levels of voters: high-income voters, 89, 90, 95, 97; low-income voters, 119; middle-income voters, 62, 94, 96
Incumbent rule on pre-election polls, 79–81, 83
Incumbents, 108–09, 111